2009

Implementing
Beyond Budgeting

Implementing Beyond Budgeting

Unlocking the Performance Potential

BJARTE BOGSNES

WILEY

John Wiley & Sons, Inc.

Published by John Wiley & Sons, Inc., Hoboken, New Jersey.
Published simultaneously in Canada.

For general information on our other products and services, or technical support,
please contact our Customer Care Department within the United States at
800-762-2974, outside the United States at 317-572-3993 or fax 317-572-4002.

Wiley also publishes its books in a variety of electronic formats. Some content
that appears in print may not be available in electronic books.

For more information about Wiley products, visit our Web site at
http://*www.wiley.com*.

Library of Congress Cataloging-in-Publication Data:

Bogsnes, Bjarte.
  Implementing beyond budgeting : unlocking the performance potential /
Bjarte Bogsnes.
    p. cm.
  Includes index.
  ISBN 978-0-470-40516-1 (cloth)
  1. Cost control.   2. Cost accounting.   3. Management.   I. Title.
  HD47.3.B64 2009
  658.15′5–dc22
                                                          2008029058

Printed in the United States of America.

10 9 8 7 6 5 4

For my wife, Tone. As a great teacher, you are the one trying to get things right from the start. The rest of us are just trying to repair.

Contents

Foreword

B jarte Bogsnes's book is an important contribution to the transformation of finance from the controlling and bean-counting office to the company's value-creating office. Bogsnes describes how to transform finance's historical role of ex post reporting and controlling into a new role that guides the enterprise forward for sustainable value creation. The transformation requires reexamining and, probably, abandoning some of the vestiges of finance's previous management control tools. In particular, several companies in Europe and North America have questioned their use of the annual operating budget, a management tool introduced at General Motors nearly a century ago by CEO Alfred Sloan and CFO Donaldson Brown. Although the operating budget was a great innovation at the time, today's dynamic and highly volatile environment has made an annual fixed operating plan an anachronism. The counterreaction to the high preparation cost, in time and money, of the annual budget and its inflexibility in light of rapidly changing external circumstances and internal opportunities has launched the Beyond Budgeting movement. Several academics and consultants have written articles and books, and led working groups of companies, about how to abandon the fixed annual budget.

The current book makes a major contribution to this movement. Unlike the previous writers, Bjarte Bogsnes has been there and done that. And not just once. Bogsnes was the intellectual and project leader at two transformational projects at major companies, Borealis and Statoil. The book draws on these rich experiences to offer practical advice about how to introduce a new set of planning and performance management systems that inspire both managers and employees to achieve break-through performance. This book is an essential read for anyone frustrated with the organization's budgeting process and look-ing to achieve the intended benefits from the budget with new systems that work better, faster, cheaper, and more flexibly. Bogsnes takes Beyond Budgeting to a new level by describing in detail the management system, "Ambition to action," that he helped introduce to replace the budget system. Along the way, he provides vivid examples of the implementation process in the two large companies that enabled them to abandon and replace a strongly embedded management system.

Bogsnes was trained in finance and worked for many years in finance organizations. He does not, however, view finance just through its typical left-brain analytic lens. Rather, he is eloquent on the importance of incorporating right-brain concepts such as trust, empowerment, leadership, transparency, and communication when designing and implementing a new management system, especially with today's workforce and competitive environment. The book is a refreshing integration of analytic left-brain concepts, including activity-based cost-ing, balanced scorecards, and performance objectives, along with vital right-brain sensitivities on motivating and leading organizational change.

I have heard Bjarte speak on many occasions. The enthu-siasm, passion, and persuasion that he exudes in person come through well in his writing. Managers searching for new ways to motivate and evaluate their people will find him inspiring, refreshing, practical, and, even, entertaining, terms not usually applied to authors of management control books.

Robert S. Kaplan
Harvard Business School
Boston, Massachusetts
June 2008

Introduction

When I first thought about writing a book about my 15-year-long journey "beyond budgeting," my immediate reaction was no. How could I possibly write 300 pages or more about something that actually is quite obvious and is basic common sense?

So please bear with me that this book is not a brick. Maybe you do not mind. Maybe there are enough bricks out there. But thank you for spending a few hours on something that is less of a story about budgets and more a story about leadership and what makes people and organizations perform and excel. The main purpose is not to get rid of budgets. Budgets are only a *barrier* that must be removed, and certainly not the only one. The main purpose is *liberation*, from dictatorship, micromanagement, number worshipping, calendar periods, hierarchies, secrecy, sticks and carrots, and all the other management myths about what is best for achieving great performance in teams and organizations. This is the regime we have to overthrow in order to make the business world a better place to live and work. Welcome to the revolution!

I hope I did not lose you with that slightly emotional outburst. Please hang on. I promise to prove the case with sober evidence and loads of practical examples. Many of these will be uncomfortably familiar.

I am a finance guy by education. My first job was actually in the Corporate Budget Department(!) in the Norwegian oil company Statoil, back in 1983. Trust me; I know the game from the inside. Not just from that job, but also from many later finance manager jobs. I have paid my dues, almost camping in my office during the frenzy of budget peak periods.

Beyond Budgeting is about leadership more than anything else. I have been in leadership roles for more than 20 years, much of the time with international and multicultural teams outside my home country, Norway. I sincerely enjoy the leadership role. It is the most challenging and rewarding job there is, after the ultimate leadership role, which of course is parenthood and raising your own children. I have tried that one as well. Our three boys are now well beyond the point of any parental influence. I think we did pretty well. Being married to a great mother and teacher was a big part of that.

I also learned about leadership in the Norwegian Army, where I spent a year at an officer school before getting to practice it all in a second year. Much of my learning was, however, about how *not* to lead, enough to abort my plans about a military career and go for business studies instead. The army has fortunately changed since I got my overdose of command and control back in the seventies.

I belong to the rather small group of finance people who have also worked in human resources (HR). I headed up an HR function for four years. I have never learned more in any other job. That period gave me invaluable inspiration and insights for the next part of my journey. First, I realized something that should be obvious, but unfortunately isn't for most Finance and HR people: Performance management cuts across their two functions, and neither of them will succeed without the other onboard. Second, I discovered the leadership side of Beyond Budgeting.

I also have the practical experience of heading up two Beyond Budgeting implementation projects in two large companies, first in Borealis and later in Statoil. Borealis was Europe's largest petrochemicals company at the time, while Statoil (now StatoilHydro) is Scandinavia's largest company. You will hear a lot more about these two projects later. I have shared my experiences from these two companies at hundreds of conferences in Europe, the United States, Asia, South America, and Australia. I have met and discussed with countless managers and professionals. There has been overwhelming and heartwarming support but also constructive challenge and pushback.

I have always been curious about what lies behind and underneath what we all observe on the surface. I have learned a lot from great stuff written on both leadership and management. This book is very much about the difference between the two. But I am also a practitioner. For me, the crossroads where theory meets practice is the place to be. When I studied business at the Norwegian School of Economics and Business Administration in my hometown of Bergen, those books did not speak to me as strongly as they do today, and not only because I perhaps was not among the most frequent visitors at the study hall. I needed the painful but rewarding experience of trying it all out in practice, where theory hits the trenches of real life. This is a story from those trenches.

Many of the issues raised in this book have been discussed before, in some form or shape. Douglas McGregor, for example, addressed many of the Beyond Budgeting leadership issues in his classic book, *The Human Side of Enterprise*, back in 1960. His "theory X and Y" is spot on. What is your fundamental belief in people? Does your sympathy lie with theory X? Do you believe that people generally dislike work and responsibility, have low ambitions, and prefer to be directed and controlled? Or do you believe the opposite, that people want to be involved, take responsibility, develop and perform, and make a positive difference? McGregor's book is timeless reading and highly recommended. He provides thoughtful insights and examples of the difference between leadership and management, and why we need so much more of the first and a lot less of the other.

The issue is not a lack of theory. There are thousands of other books and articles to draw from. The knowledge is out there. What we need is all of that theory to be put to work. We need to see radical change in the millions of organizations and teams where old-fashioned management is executed every day. Theory X is alive and kicking as if nothing has happened over the last 50 years.

One label for what this book is about could be performance management. My problem is that I really don't like that phrase. The "performance" word is great; it is the combination with "management" I struggle with. How do you feel if someone tells you they are going to "manage your performance"? I know what my response is. My defense system immediately goes on red alert. Nobody is going to mess around in my head! Nobody is going to pull my strings as if I am some kind of dancing marionette!

You will still at times catch me using the phrase, because I have yet to find a better one. A more appropriate label might be organizational behavior. Unfortunately, many of those we need to reach with the Beyond Budgeting message immediately switch off when they hear such soft and nonfinancial words. Until we find a better name, I am afraid "performance management" will have to do. Please let me know if you have a better proposal!

In fact, I do not believe that performance really can be "managed" at all, at least not in the traditional way so many management theories want us to believe. People are not robots and organizations are not machines. We cannot just sit in the control room, pull the strings, push the buttons, and "manage" performance.

What we *can* do is to create the *conditions* needed for good performance to take place. We can create an environment of trust and transparency, of motivating challenge and stretch, of care and support, where people perform because they want to, not because they are told to. But this is all we can do. People are not marionettes. They can choose to respond to these conditions, but they cannot be forced, they cannot be "managed." People feel *underled* and *overmanaged*. They are hungry for good leadership: direction, inspiration, and support. Good leaders should create *clarity, capability*, and *commitment*. Direction on which mountain to climb, and the ability and wish to get up there. That is leadership in a nutshell, and also very much what Beyond Budgeting is about. It is not so much the actual budget as a *product* we are after as the *mind-set* that budgeting represents. It is the myths and beliefs of traditional management we need to fight. It is theory X again, that unless people are kept on short leashes and tightly controlled, they will all run away and do stupid things. It is the blind belief that good performance is all about hitting those budget numbers. It is the naiveté of believing that if we only describe the future to enough decimal places, then we know what will happen and can safely set sail. It is the myth that throwing money at people is the best or the only way to motivate. It is the belief that as long as we can explain, we are in control.

Control is the mantra. If we stick to our beliefs, we might get "control." But do we really get the best possible performance? Control is such an important word and such a big part of the management agenda that we need to address it already now. When managers are asked about their biggest concern in abandoning traditional management practices, including budgeting, invariably the answer is "losing control." When asked to be a bit more specific, they all continue with "losing cost control." When asked what else they mean by the word "control," everybody agrees the list is much longer but most struggle with providing specific examples for the controls they would be jeopardizing. Some talk about "avoiding deviations"; they dislike the real world taking a route other than planned. Some mention avoiding people making too many decisions on their own.

Others might say "understanding what is happening," which makes sense. But generally, they struggle. They all insist that control goes beyond cost control, but few can immediately name exactly how, even if it is what they fear to lose the most! I find this quite fascinating.

You might be struggling to put a finger on this as well, so let us sort this out right away. There is some control we want to keep and some control we want to get rid of. We still want to understand where we have been and where we are, through quality accounting and reporting. We still need effective processes and order in the house. We still need to understand when we are performing well and when we are not. These kinds of controls have nothing to fear from Beyond Budgeting; on the contrary.

There are, however, two other types of control that we want less of. The first one is *controlling* what people shall and shall not do, through detailed budgets, tight mandates, detailed job descriptions, rigid organizational structures, smartly constructed bonus schemes, and all other control mechanisms honed through decades of believing in and practicing this kind of management.

The second type of control, we probably never had to begin with. That is the perceived control of the future, the one we think we get if we only have enough numbers and details in our plans and forecasts. The business environment keeps getting more complex, turbulent, and unpredictable. We try to cope with all the complexity by *simplifying*. Once we have reduced it all to one voluminous and single outcome set of numbers, it all seems more orderly and manageable. This perceived control we carry with us when tomorrow becomes today, and we feel at least somewhat in control when we can explain in detail where and why we once again got it wrong. If we, however, do hit our numbers, we absolutely feel "in control." But did we really get the best possible performance?

Some of the fear of losing control probably comes from the term "Beyond Budgeting" itself. The headline always runs faster than the rest of the story. As a stand-alone label, many believe the term stands for anarchy and unlimited spending. People usually calm down when they get the full picture. When they understand *why* we are abolishing budgets and other worn-out management practices, and what we do instead, most agree that it makes sense, even if they still have some questions and concerns. Most people also relax somewhat when they understand that we will continue doing the good things a budget *tries* to do for us but fails so miserably with (I will explain why in the next chapter). We will still set motivating *targets*, provide good *forecasts*, and secure an effective allocation of scarce *resources*.

Traditional management, budgets, and even theory X might have worked better in the past. It is not true that everything practiced in earlier days necessarily was wrong and ineffective. But things have changed. That was a different time. The main challenge was to produce enough to meet a bottomless demand. The performance pressure was lower. People were less educated. Social norms about masters and servants were stronger. What lies ahead of us is, however, very different from what lies behind us. We are sailing into new and unknown waters. The winds and the currents are shifting faster and much more unexpectedly than before. The weather forecasts and our maps are no longer as reliable as they used to be. Sometimes we even have to sail without them. We need to be on a continuous lookout and act fast when the wind turns or a reef appears out of nowhere. And it does not stop here. In these troubled waters, we are also expected to sail even faster than before. And last but not least, the crew has expectations and capabilities that go way beyond blindly accepting orders from the captain. The ability to sense and respond *together* has never been more critical.

When sailing in these new waters, we need *less* traditional management and *more* leadership, less theory X and more theory Y. This is the only way to mobilize the maximum performance from everyone onboard. This is the only way to not just safely reach the next harbor, but also to be there first, not among the battered and beaten last ones.

Mobilizing that maximum performance requires reaching the untapped potential in people that far too often lies unrecognized and untouched during working hours. Sometimes it only takes a change of clothes to wake it up. When the cap reads "volunteer," "coach," or "kitchen refurbisher," people's abilities often go far beyond what companies are able to reach.

This untapped potential is much larger than what even the most hard-selling management consultant will dare to promise. Think back on all the different managers you have had throughout your career. Include your teachers at school or at university, and perhaps your parents as well. Think about the best one, and what that person was able to get out of you in terms of learning, development, and performance. It is probably a warm memory. Then try to recall the worst one. This one is often harder to bring back. We have buried those faces and voices deep, to avoid them ever turning up again. If you found him or her, think about the performance—or rather the lack of performance—that person was able to get out of you. In my own case, the difference is *huge*. Yours is probably quite big too.

But compared to the performance delta companies need to mobilize in order to compete and win today, the additional performance available from you and I can be overlooked. But the two of us are not special. This potential, which can be reached only by those very best leaders, exists in everyone. Imagine if our "deltas" are multiplied not just by 2, but by a number equal to all the people in the organization, 100, or 100,000. Then the impact and importance of good leadership becomes real and massive. Can we really afford to leave something of this magnitude untouched and untapped?

There might have been no journey to write about if it was not for Svein Rennemo, perhaps the best leader I ever had—among quite a few great ones. I was reporting to Svein when I headed up Corporate Control (what a terrible name, and I picked it myself!) in the newly formed European petrochemicals company Borealis back in the mid-1990s. Svein was the CFO and later the CEO of Borealis. You will hear a lot more about this company later.

"What do you expect from us?" That was the question I asked him back in 1995, when Borealis was undertaking a full-blown business process reengineering, which is (or was) consultancy language for "leave no stone unturned and look for a better way." I was asked to head up a part of this project called "Management Effectiveness," and I was quite uncertain about what kind of content to put behind this name. So I asked Svein what he really expected from us. I will never forget his response. He looked at me with his mild and kind eyes, which I knew should never be mistaken for a lack of determination or a will of steel. Smilingly, he said to me: "Bjarte, I expect the unexpected." That was all. So much challenge, and so much trust, in so few words.

Triggered by that message, some months later we decided to abolish budgeting in Borealis. For me, those words from a great leader became the start of a long journey. Or maybe the journey started even earlier, among a group of newly appointed and very exhausted Borealis controllers. Exhausted because we had made two budgets in one year during the 1994 start-up, on top of a very intense integration process. This group of extremely tired people spent their last drop of energy on a "lessons learned" day, discussing how to improve the Borealis budgeting process. The outcome of that day was not very impressive. One short but ignored question was, however, the seed of something that none of us in the room recognized, not until several months later.

You will hear more about that important day when we re-
visit the Borealis case. Before that, we have to start with all
the problems caused by traditional management. We will do
that in Chapter 1, where we discuss how traditional management has become more of a barrier than a support for good
performance, and how we also end up with low quality and
low efficiency in the performance management process itself.
The budget is one of the problems, but certainly not the only
one. We review serious and often overlooked problems related
to trust, cost management, rhythm, target setting, performance
evaluation, bonus, quality, and efficiency. In Chapter 2 we look
at the Beyond Budgeting model. First we review the general
model and then we visit the Beyond Budgeting Round Table,
before making the concept more tangible by taking a look at the
famous Handelsbanken case. This Swedish bank made radical
changes to its performance management model back in 1970
and is a great reference case when moving to Borealis and Statoil in Chapters 3 and 4. The Borealis case is a story from the
1990s, while the Statoil case is a fresh field report from an ongoing journey, where maps and directions keep changing even
as this book is written. I also share seven balanced scorecard
pitfalls to watch out for, since the scorecard is a key ingredient
in the new models of both companies. In Chapter 5 I share
what I have learned from heading up both of these Beyond
Budgeting projects. I take you through seven implementation
best practices coming straight out of the real world, including
several mistakes we made.

Before we move on, I need to issue a warning. Throughout
this book, you will often find me shouting. You will probably feel that I from time to time make things quite black and
white, when for instance criticizing the budget and the damage
it causes.

I do this on purpose, and with no guilt, because I am convinced there is something fundamentally wrong. That starting

point is nonnegotiable. "Capital letters" or not, I simply want to make sure that at least some of my worries and warnings about traditional management come through. If I succeed, I also want to offer help and a way out of the misery. As a minimum, I want to leave you with an uneasy feeling that perhaps there is something to this. I do, however, have high hopes. I believe most of you will agree with most of what I have to say, because it is nothing but common sense.

Acknowledgments

A wise person once said that if you want to travel fast, travel alone. If you want to travel far, travel together. I want to thank all my fellow travelers on this long journey. There are so many of you.

In Statoil, a special thank you goes to:

- Eldar Sætre, for creating the foundation and securing the green light
- Torgrim Reitan, for unlimited trust and support
- Arvid Hollevik, for all the energy, for the great discussions, and for backing it all with a wonderful system
- My colleagues and all of you out in the business, taking this into your own units. I dare not list names, because there are so many of you. You know who you are!
- My Human Resource colleagues. Together we can be dynamite!

I am deeply in debt to all my friends at the Beyond Budgeting Round Table, especially Jeremy Hope, Robin Fraser, Steve Morlidge, Peter Bunce, Franz Röösli, and Steve Player. If it wasn't for you guys . . . .

Dag Larsson at EKAN has been there for more than 20 years, with his big open questions triggering all those important discussions.

Thank you to Thomas Boesen in Borealis for keeping the spirit alive in the Finance function after I moved to Human

Resources, and to everybody else in the Finance team, especially Gunnar Nielsen, Asbjørn Holte, and Anders Frøberg. I am also grateful for all the support and patience from my Borealis HR colleagues.

Tim Burgard and Lisa Vuoncino at Wiley: Your advice and support have been both needed and appreciated!

A special thank you to Bob Kaplan for all the enthusiasm and invaluable support!

And last but not least, Svein Rennemo: Thank you for the push, the challenge, and the trust. Not everybody dares to expect the unexpected. You did.

CHAPTER 1

Problems with Traditional Management

Introduction

In this chapter, we take a closer look at the many problems with traditional management, which I have only been hinting at so far. This is where we have to start. If there are no problems, why should we bother changing? Why fix something that is not broken? If we do not agree on the serious damage traditional management can cause, there is no common ground to build a new model on. There has to be a case for change.

Some of the problems with traditional management are directly linked to budgets and budgeting. Others are more indirectly linked, but often rooted in the budgeting mind-set of command and control.

Let us start with the budget. It is not the only problem, but it is a major one. Over the last 15 years, I have asked thousands of managers, in Borealis, in Statoil, and in hundreds of other companies what they think of the budgeting process. It is just like pushing a button. Everybody has a view. The response is loud and clear. The vast majority of people are critical, and many are extremely negative. The examples and stories people share vary, however, quite a lot. They typically list negative experiences within their own area of work. In sales, production, research, or administration, people often see quite different problems with how budgets and budgeting affect their jobs. Many see the main problem as all of the time and energy spent on budgets. Some feel it constrains them from doing the right things and a good job. Others are concerned about how meaningless the budget can be as a yardstick in performance evaluation.

Although most people are well aware of isolated symptoms, few see a bigger picture. One thing they all have in common, however, is a scary cynicism about the whole process in itself as well as the people behind it: the "bean counters" and "stupid managers" and all the other honest feedback you get in private conversations. When so many are so critical, why have more companies not radically challenged and transformed their budgeting process? Where is the revolution, when there is so much dissatisfaction boiling among the people?

I believe the main reason for lack of major change is a missing diagnosis. Many see the budget problems as an irritating itch but not as a dangerous disease. The local and often diverse problem descriptions do not easily translate into a broader and more structural problem. Although the symptoms are easily recognized, the disease is not. And even if some do sense or see the shades of a bigger budget problem, they are often unable to connect this to *other* weaknesses in the management model, such as a deep and hierarchical organization structure, lack of transparency, or a culture of fear and submission.

Some companies, however, see patterns and realize that something more serious is wrong. For these companies, the barrier to change might be the lack of an alternative. Leaving old and well-tested practices, including abolishing the budget, is considered an unthinkable paradigm shift. "Of course we know that much of what we do isn't very smart or doesn't work very well, but what should we do instead?" they wonder. Beyond Budgeting answers that question. The concept provides not just a comprehensive diagnosis but also advice on how to cure the serious disease that so many organizations are suffering from.

Our blind faith in traditional management is holding us back. It is time to challenge these myths that have dominated management thinking and driven management practices for far too long. These myths are firm beliefs like:

- No centralized control = Chaos and anarchy
- Good performance = Hitting the budget numbers
- No budget = Cost explosion
- No individual bonus = No performance
- More details = More quality
- Need to know = Enough to know
- I can explain = I have control

You might hesitate to buy into this massive attack on traditional management and budgets without any supporting evidence. If you are skeptical, I hope we at least can agree that any process should from time to time be reviewed and pressure-tested. There is always a better way. It is wise to have a regular medical checkup even if you do not feel sick. So if your guard is up right now, please let it down during the next pages, while we examine more in depth whether we have a problem or not. I promise to provide hard evidence.

Which Way in a New Business Environment?

What is it that really drives good performance in organizations? What is it that makes people get up in the morning, go to work, wanting to do their best? How do we get the best possible results? How do we sense and respond faster than the competition? How do we release creativity and innovation? Why should people work for us and not someone else?

These kinds of questions have probably been asked from the very early days of organizations and leadership. The *questions* are the same. It is the *answers* that have changed. The old answers were quite simple, and included strong doses of hierarchical command and control. Many of these answers probably did work well in the past. But the business world has changed radically since the days of Taylor, T Fords, and Threat management.

Across almost all businesses, the operating environment has become radically more dynamic, unpredictable, and turbulent. In addition, the performance expectations from customers, shareholders, and other stakeholders have also increased dramatically. So has the transparency of business. There are few places to hide anymore. Both the *need* for and the *expectations* for outstanding performance have never been higher.

It is almost as if we have been through a "global warming" of the entire business climate. The "climate changes" are faster, more unpredictable, and more violent than in those reliable and quiet summers and winters we recall from our happy childhoods. Just look at the volatility of oil prices. Many businesses, not just oil companies, have oil price as a key variable in their business performance. We try to make short- and long-term projections, and we all fail miserably. We simply do not know anymore. Look at the pace of technological innovation. Making a five-year business plan for a record company today must be a nightmare compared to the good old days before new digital formats and downloading. And why should it stop here?

The real global warming still has its skeptics, but no one seems to dispute this one. The evidence of change is everywhere. We are almost overwhelmed with uncertainty. The only thing that has become *more* certain is that our predictions about what lies ahead most likely are wrong. The future has become less "plannable." Whether we like it or not, "the future ain't what it used to be," as the American baseball player Yogi Berra once put it.

At the same time, life *inside* organizations has also changed dramatically. The massive difference between market value and book value in companies might be the most tangible proof that something has happened. The value of human capital, innovation, creativity, and people's desire to contribute and make a difference is often the only value that exists, and it can walk out the door any day. Actually it does, every afternoon, often becoming even more valuable because people then reveal additional talents. Employees do not see themselves as "workers" in such organizations, and they cannot be managed as "workers." They have different and higher expectations than earlier generations. Traditional management struggles when people regard leadership as something that must be earned and not assigned through stars and stripes.

As Gary Hamel says in his great book, *The Future of Management*, traditional management was invented to ensure an effective *replication*, from T Fords to Pentium chips. Today, it seems to have lost even that hegemony. Toyota now churns out cars faster and better than any other manufacturer in the world, because it did not adopt everything coming from the West after World War II. The company seems to lead and operate in a way the competition apparently is not. At Toyota, anyone working on the production line has the authority to make the very costly decision to stop the line if necessary. Likely this occurs very seldom, but simply *knowing* that you have the authority does something to how you feel about your job and your company.

At Semco, a Brazilian company that seems to have challenged every single myth of traditional management, all employees have the right to attend any meeting (with a few exceptions). They do not, but they know they can. I read *Maverick* 20 years ago, the first book by their CEO, Ricardo Semler. His story made a deep impression on me, and both his books are highly recommended.

These are examples of practices that one by one should be quite easy to copy. At both Toyota and Semco, these and many other practices seem together to form a holistic alternative to traditional management that is much more difficult to copy. Western car manufacturers have been studying and benchmarking Toyota for decades, and they are still scratching their heads. Perhaps one reason is that the old management mind-set still is so strong that they have not even attempted to replace it, so they end up with a bit of Japanese wisdom on top of and not instead of the good old way. As we discuss later, there is no simpler and more painless way to change than to add instead of replace. The only problem is that you get very little change.

If we agree that today there exists a radically new business climate, where the winds and waves are hammering the boat more viciously than ever, where expectations for sailing faster and for finding new routes and new land are increasing by the day, and where everyone in the crew expects to have a hand on the rudder and an eye on the map, then it should not be difficult to agree that there must be consequences. Whether we are in oil, cars, music, or any other business, this new climate must have *some* kind of implications for how we lead and manage. In such radically different circumstances, we cannot just keep sailing as before. The issue cannot be *if* a change is needed, but *which* change. In which direction, and how big?

Companies are not deaf and blind. Most do respond, but in very different ways. Some go for a fine-tuning only of their management processes. This typically means no real change at all, just a bit of singing and dancing: hiring consultants to help introduce some of the latest music in the charts, simplifying the budget process by asking for a little bit less than last year, in addition to the inevitable reshuffling of the organizational chart. Others are more serious and might already have tried some of the medicine mentioned. They believe the answer lies in "much more of what we already do." Their response is to pull harder and tougher on existing management levers. They go for longer budget processes, more analysis, more number-crunching, tougher budget interventions and instructions from above, with more negotiations and gaming, tighter budget follow-up, and higher bonuses for achieving budget targets. The strategy is simple: more of the old answers, more micromanagement and command and control in order to get back into the "control" they had or thought they had in the past.

This is a tempting strategy for many. It also represents a major paradox. The more uncertainty and turbulence and the more urgent need there is to break with the past and go for radical change, the stronger the fear of letting go and leaving what is perceived as a safe and calm harbor in stormy weather, namely those familiar and well-tested management practices, including the good old budget.

Not everybody responds like this. A small but growing group of companies realize that the answer neither lies in fine-tuning nor in radically increasing the doses of current medication. They realize that the disease requires a radically different lifestyle. They believe in moving in the *opposite* direction. They believe that in this new business climate, teams and people need *more* and not less room to move. They trust their people to make the right decisions when the hurricane hits or when they face any other unexpected situation that seldom can be foreseen in a budget made a year and a half earlier. They understand that business is continuous, with individual rhythms that seldom match the calendar year. They understand the need for a broader and more intelligent performance language. They appreciate that not all wisdom sits at the top. These companies understand that their leadership must be built *on* and not *against* human nature. They question every single myth in traditional management.

In the sections that follow, I explain which problems these companies have identified and understood and why they are rebelling. These problems include:

- Trust
- Cost management
- Target setting and evaluation
- Bonus
- Rhythm
- Quality
- Efficiency

The Trust Problem

Companies going in that opposite direction all have *trust* as a key ingredient in their leadership philosophy and their performance management process. Trust is perhaps the most important word in the Beyond Budgeting vocabulary. No one should consider leaving existing practices before being clear about where they stand on this one.

Where do you stand?

Do you believe that without tight control and short leashes, detailed budgets and sharp instructions, the organization will drift into anarchy where people will do all kinds of stupid things and spend money like drunken sailors? If that is your belief, you have a *really* serious problem, but probably not with your organization. If you hardly trust anyone and believe you are the only responsible person around, then maybe your problem rests much more with yourself than with anyone else.

Few would admit to thinking like this. Actually, I believe most managers do trust most of their people. So the starting point is the right one, and also the only one you can have. But what happens with this trust when we move from what we say to what we actually *practice* in our performance management processes? Then trust has a tendency to disappear, only to be replaced with a very different word. That word is *control*.

It is quite a paradox how "western" business leaders praise democracy as the obvious and undisputable model for how to organize a society effectively. When the same leaders turn to their own companies, then their beliefs and inspiration seem to come from a very different place, from the very opposite ideologies. Traditional management has more in common with old Soviet Union–style centralized planning and control than with the principles and beliefs of a true democracy. In democratic societies, we take for granted that we elect our own leaders, that everybody has a voice, that discussion and disagreement drives us forward, that information is open and free-flowing, and that big decisions are taken in referendums. We smile about the hopeless socialist idea of making centralized and detailed five-year plans instead of letting the market sort it out. It is a no-brainer that there cannot be a monopoly but a choice of capital sources open all year to fund new ideas and start-ups. This is what we preach and practice as members of a free society.

But what happens when we put that other hat on? When we go to work and become managers or employees in companies, none of this seems so obvious anymore. We seem to surrender at the company gates all the trust and freedom we take for granted as citizens. The trust that managers have and people expect evaporates like hot summer rain when the scene changes from society to company. And worse, we hardly seem to question it.

Why does this happen? Why do employees surrender so easily what they take for granted as citizens? Many seem to be on autopilot, stuck in the same traditional management patterns as their bosses. Maybe some do not quite like it, but they accept it as the way things always have been. In many societies, democracy has a short history. The old regimes had perhaps less of this paradox, because the situation was very much the same on both sides of the company gates.

All of this is changing, and not only in political systems around the world. Young people who question the old ways vote with their feet as they are drawn toward companies that dare to challenge the past, that want to tear down that Berlin Wall between democracy and company principles.

What about the managers? They are also stuck in tradition and old habits. Many of them have built their careers on mastering traditional management. They actually might be in their current positions because they are very good at this way of managing. They also get support for sticking to old beliefs from the behavior of *some* people in the organization. Any organization has people who are either too smart or too immature to deserve or handle trust and freedom. You have them in your organization too. I am sure you can even name a few. Although we know they are few, and even if we do trust the large majority of people in the organization, far too often we let this small minority drive our leadership thinking and the design of our performance management models. We give people tight mandates and detailed budgets that are nothing but straitjackets. We issue instructions clearly aimed at the few but knowing they will apply to everyone. We do so because there might be *someone* who cannot be trusted. The strategy seems to be preventive control on everybody instead of damage control on those few.

It cannot be this way. If we trust most of our people, that big majority must be the design platform for our models rather than the small minority. At the same time, we shall not be naive. The minority is a reality that we must face and not ignore. We must be crystal clear on our values and performance standards. We need mechanisms that can reveal unacceptable behaviors and help catch these guys, and we must act decisively when trust is misused. And I mean *when*, not *if*, because it will happen.

Our reaction must, however, *not* be a retreat back to the old way because "Trust does not work." The pressure will come, from the theory X supporters and all those longing back to the simpler days of command and control: "What did we say? We warned you! This trust thing will never work!" Do not let them push you. Deal swiftly with incidents, but do not let them drive you back. Exceptions must not be generalized. In a democracy, we do not lock up all potential criminals because someone some day might do something wrong. But we have clear boundaries, and crossing the line has consequences.

If the entire management model reeks of mistrust and control mechanisms against unwanted behavior, the result might actually be more, not less, of what we try to prevent. The more people are treated as criminals, the more we risk that they will behave as such.

If you still insist on a mistrust-based control approach, you are moving into a war with no end. People will always find ways of cheating if they really want to. Their motivation will be fueled by your behavior and your controls, and vice versa. It is a vicious circle and a lose-lose game.

In both Borealis and Statoil, the skeptics asked us again and again: What will prevent people from uncontrolled spending if we drop the budgets? Can we really trust these guys to manage their own costs? It was their concern number one, two, and three. But what kind of people were we actually talking about? It was people we trusted with building or working on million- and billion-dollar machines: crackers, pipelines, offshore platforms, oil refineries. It was people we trusted with trading crude oil or handling currency exposures for millions every single day. But manage their own travel costs? Are you kidding?

A good friend of mine is a pilot and captain with a large international airline. Despite the huge responsibility he is entrusted with, both people's lives and expensive airplanes, he still needs a written approval if he wants to change his uniform

shirt more frequently than what is stated in the uniform procedures.

If we cannot trust these guys on the small things, how can
we really trust them on the big things? Could it be that we are
more concerned about what we understand (such as travel costs
or shirt cleaning) than about what most of us understand less
of (such as running a refinery or flying an airplane)? Many of
these line managers have other financial targets on top of cost
budgets—for instance, profitability or unit cost targets. Under
these targets, they cannot spend more unless they produce more
or sell more. But this self-regulating mechanism is obviously not
sufficient; we also have to micromanage. No wonder there is a
lot of cynicism around.

The less managers trust others, the more they may think
about themselves and their own capabilities or heightened self-
esteems. Often these same managers are the ones who cannot
make a decision without calling in armies of management consultants because they do not trust their own judgment. These
same managers litter their language and communication with
buzzwords and the latest management jargon because they do
not trust the power of their own plain English.

Lack of trust often goes hand in hand with lack of transparency. If you do not trust people, it is logical to also restrict
the information they have access to. "Nice to know" is of course
far too much access. Need to know, as defined at the top, is
seen as more than enough. Traditional management offers several effective ways of restricting information. The organizational
hierarchy is one favorite. The deeper the better, and even better
if there are no horizontal leaks over to neighboring structures
as selected information is passed down the chain of command,
filtered as necessary at each level.

Then we have our performance management systems,
which sometimes come with more filters than some governments have available for blocking undesirable Web sites. Instead

of believing that everything should be open, and closed only where strictly needed, it is often the other way around. Another internal information channel, the company intranet, also has a certain Orwellian atmosphere in many companies, trying to give us that "Shiny Happy People" feeling. Many company home pages would benefit greatly both in trustworthiness and usefulness by turning down somewhat the one-way aren't-we-great messages. Instead, we need much more employee-driven discussions and information exchange. Why are there, for instance, so few internal company blogs when the external world is full of them? We need more two-way communication, sharing constructive challenge and dialogue on all the work-related issues that people want to discuss and improve. But there seems to be a fear among senior managers (and among communication people) of people speaking up, of critical viewpoints that might fit badly with the image companies try to paint of themselves. The parallel is found in totalitarian regimes more than in those democracies we want to be our models.

So far, we seem to have used technology mainly to *automate* our traditional internal communication. Instead, we need to change it into something that perhaps is not more radical than what people meet when they walk out the company gates and log into cyberspace on their company-sponsored home PCs.

There is actually a major paradox here. Traditional management fears transparency because it threatens control. But as Jeremy Hope, cofounder of the Beyond Budgeting Round Table, puts it, "Transparency *is* the new control system." There is a reason why thieves and crooks prefer to operate at night. Maybe Enron would have been in existence today if there had been more transparency. When everybody can see what everybody spends and how everybody performs, it does something no formal control system is able to deliver.

It is easier to talk about trust than to practice it. Some of you might not even want to go close to what is recommended here, because you are too uncomfortable with the implications, or maybe because you simply disagree. But do you actually have a choice? Think about "global warming," the speed of change, and all the uncertainty surrounding us. The enlightened emperor making all decisions on behalf of the common people in the dark is not just old-fashioned thinking; it is simply not possible anymore. Whether you like it or not, you have to let go in more and more management arenas where you used to be king of the road. You have to take the backseat more often and let the front-line people read the maps; find the quickest route; and do the driving, turning, speeding, and braking. But do not worry; there is more than enough left for you to do in the backseat, including setting direction, coaching, motivating, and assisting when needed. Just do not become a backseat driver!

I love my parents. They have always trusted me, even when I did not deserve it. In their generation, there seldom was more than one driver's license in the family. Driving was a man's job. It would not have been easy for my father, or any other man of that generation, to let go if my mother had gotten a license as well. I do not think he was too comfortable the few times I did the driving either, even if he never said so. But those were different days. Today, almost everybody can drive. You do not have to do all the driving yourself. Lean back, trust the driver, and *lead* instead!

The Cost Management Problem

The most stubborn myth in traditional management is probably that the only way to manage cost is through detailed cost budgets, with a tight follow-up to ensure that no more is spent than is handed out. Without such tight controls, money will be wasted and costs will explode.

The cost management problem is not the most serious one, but I have chosen to address it early. The consequences of removing cost budgets is what worries managers the most when they cautiously ask themselves "Could this work in our company?" or firmly concluding "This would never work in our company! We can't let things completely loose. Maybe budgets lead to suboptimal behaviors, but isn't that a price worth paying for keeping costs under control? Our people are not mature enough for this!" It is the *trust* problem again, as we discussed in the previous section. But beyond the trust issue, there are also a number of *other* reasons why traditional budgets are no longer the most effective way of securing an efficient use of resources. Let us take a look at these.

A cost budget is a kind of *ceiling* we put on cost: "This is how much you can spend and no more." In most companies, this ceiling seems to work quite well. It is simple to communicate and easy to track. Tight follow-up combined with a surprisingly high level of budget loyalty, given all the cynicism, typically results in actual cost coming in around budget, year after year. Great performance! What is the problem? The ceiling works, we do not spend more than decided. We have costs under control, have we not?

Yes, we have, if this is how we define control, if the goal is to spend no more than decided 15 to 16 months ago. But is this really what we aim for? Are we not after an *efficient* and *value-creating* use of resources, even if that should cost somewhat more or somewhat less than decided last year?

Let us take a look at what actually takes place here. We forget that the ceiling also works just as well and often better as a *floor* for the same costs. Cost budgets tend to be spent, even when the initial budget assumptions change (which they almost always do). Managers do not necessarily behave like this to cheat; they do it because the system encourages them to do so. Managers see budgets as *entitlements*, as bags of money handed out at the beginning of the year. Nobody gets fired for spending their budget. Spending too much is, of course, bad, but spending too little is not good either. Why did you ask for more money than you really needed? It is not very smart either, if you want to protect next year's budget.

When a bag of budget money is handed out each autumn, an artificial border of concern is created. As long as we are well within budget, we spend "our" money with a good conscience and few concerns. Why should we not? We got that bag from someone who is supposed to be a wise and competent person, our manager at the next higher level, did we not?

When we finally start to see the bottom of the bag, the concern starts to creep in. Now we finally start asking ourselves: "Should we really do this? Is this wise use of money?" These questions, which seldom are heard in January, are far too important to be asked in November and December only. They need to be asked all the time, from the first penny spent.

Another problem is that not only *one* bag is handed out. We are talking about huge mountains of bags. Each department gets its own, with a lot of smaller bags inside, "because we cannot just give you one big bag of money!" These smaller bags are labeled salary, overtime, travel, consultants, and so on, which then are split into even smaller monthly bags. There is actually some trust involved, because this last part we are sometimes allowed to do ourselves.

We end up with a budget close to or sometimes even equal to the accounting detail level (same accounts, cost centers, periods, etc.). Even in smaller companies with a few hundred cost centers and around 30 to 40 budgeted cost accounts, thousands of bags are handed out each year. In bigger companies, the number probably is hundreds of thousands. Fortunately, no physical packaging is required; otherwise the environmental impact would be a disaster. There is also a lot of work involved in negotiating what we believe is the right size on all of these bags every year. But if there are no surprises, no new opportunities, and no change in assumptions ahead, the problem could have stopped here. But it does not.

Combine this detailed allocation of money with the "global warming" and all the uncertainty about what lies around the next corner. How do we know, up to a year and a half in advance, exactly what the right and optimal cost level should be? Not just the right total amount, but also exactly how much to put into each of all those bags? What kind of insight into the future do we think we have?

"But I can just reallocate between the bags if things happen," you might say. Well, you are half right. You can give people more money, but just try to do the opposite; try to *reduce* the budget for someone during the year. You will be met with a thousand arguments for why this cannot be done, and what kind of disasters will happen if you try. It is the entitlement effect: "It is my money!"

The budget might be detailed and it might tie people's hands and feet, but at least it helps us to manage the cost pressure boiling in the organization, right? Well, really? What happens during the autumn budget negotiations? As the budget approving manager, you are presented with a long list of great new activities and projects. All of them are so good that you feel like a Californian Terminator once you start challenging or cutting. What you do not get, however, is that other list, the one of finalized activities and projects that would have pulled the need for resources in the opposite direction. And then there is inflation and contingencies. When the year starts, it does not take long before the first application for additional funds comes in, backed by convincing arguments and a strong business case. But do we ever see the opposite take place during the year, managers knocking on your door wanting to give money back because you gave them too much? The number of budget reductions and increases during the year should over time balance. In practice, it is a one-way exercise.

As the budget-approving manager, this is a game you are bound to lose. You will always have less information than the unit itself about the real need for resources, status on ongoing activities and projects, and quality of new projects. "But I am the boss," you might say. "I can just cut the crap and decide on their budget for next year." Yes, you can. But do not forget the "global warming." With all that uncertainty, and with less knowledge of the business than the unit itself, how do *you* know what the right number is? You can just add a percentage for inflation, you say. Yes, you can, and so can a monkey.

To make sure that money is spent from the right bag, there is also the detailed monthly follow-up of actual costs against the year-to-date budget (the one we were trusted to make ourselves). Deviations are spotted with accounting accuracy. Never mind the fact that our monthly reference point becomes more and more obsolete and irrelevant as months go by, assumptions change, and the real world moves on. We calculate and analyze, and then another budget myth kicks in. *We can explain*. We know where the deviations are, and even why. We have control. Mission complete!

The word "cost" is also interesting. "Cost" is an accounting term for how a financial transaction should be classified and treated. Cost is something negative; it is something we must deduct from our revenues. It reduces our results. For *internal* performance management purposes, we should, however, distinguish between two types of costs: *good* costs and *bad* costs. Good costs are actually investments, which accounting rules require us to classify as costs. You spend money but you get more back. As long as we have the financial and organizational capacity, good costs are something we want more of, because they create value. It is the bad costs we want to get rid of, because they are less generous; they destroy value by giving less back than we put in.

This brings us to another major weakness with traditional cost budgeting: The focus is typically on what we put in, not on what we get back. It is a myopic way of managing costs. Take variable production cost. What is more interesting, how much we spend in total, or how much we spend per unit? Is it bad to spend more if we produce more? Would we not expect less cost if we produce less? Unit cost says much more about efficiency and performance because it addresses both sides of the equation, both input and output.

Another mantra is *low* costs. We want costs as low as possible. Cutting budgets is the way to achieve just that. But what we want is not necessarily the *lowest* possible cost level. What we want is the *optimal* cost level, the one that maximizes value creation. How do we know what that optimal level is? Of course it is difficult to find. But turn it around. How do we know what the right *lowest* cost level is? Is it zero? Is it half of current level? Two-thirds? It is just as difficult to find the right lowest cost level as it is to find the right optimal one. But let us at least agree that it is the optimal cost level we are after and that it is bad costs we want to get rid of.

Let us move to a slightly different resource issue. Our planning and resource allocation processes are based on the assumption that *financial capital* is the major constraint. We have established a common and well-understood language for reporting on and managing this scarce resource, and we are able to classify actual or planned spending down to the last penny. When new projects are evaluated and prioritized against expected financial capacity, we are able to describe in detail how we think these will draw on and later contribute to our financial resources.

In an increasing number of businesses, however, financial capital is no longer the main constraint or the main asset.

Human capital gradually is taking this role. Our planning and resource allocation processes struggle with this shift. Finance has spent decades perfecting the financial language, through common charts of accounts; international financial reporting standards; and systems for data capture, reporting, and audit. Human resources (HR), however, is still in the very early days of trying to do something similar with human capital. We do not even have a common vocabulary for describing this kind of capital, and no systems and processes to collect such information. Our records might tell us how many employees we have, their ages, education, and job history. But this is a pretty thin language for describing our most important asset. What do we really know about people's competence, about their skills and knowledge? How can we talk about filling competence gaps when we hardly know what we have and struggle with describing what we need? In budgets and business plans, this key resource is reduced to a headcount only, and often we struggle even to get that counting right.

Some companies are trying to establish common competence languages. The intention is good, but the result is often a range of languages, with limited possibility for a meaningful communication internally or with external stakeholders. Just imagine if the outside world had to relate to companies that all described their financial situation differently, through local languages developed in-house, without any common, agreed, and audited way of sharing the information.

This is an area where finance can help. The purpose is not to reduce competence mapping to a detailed and mechanical accounting exercise, but some structure and rigor is needed. Some of the principles applied on the finance side are highly relevant and could be adopted by HR.

Let us return to the cost management issue and address questions many of you probably have been jumping in your chairs to ask during these pages: "What if you are in a business where margins are counted in fractions of a cent? What if the financial situation is so bad that tight cost management is a question of life or death? It is easy to abolish budgets in an oil company drowning in cash!" Well, actually we are not swimming in money. The recent cost increases on drilling rigs, steel, engineering, and almost all other elements in our cost base does not leave much of the oil price increase in our pockets. In addition, governments across the world have increased oil company taxation. But that is another story. The question is still relevant and deserves an answer.

Borealis was by no means a "rich" company. Red numbers were no stranger to us, and tight and constantly falling margins were the name of the game. Still, all the problems with traditional cost budgets that I just have discussed were highly relevant also in such a business. The cost budget was just as much a floor as a ceiling. The concern questions were asked too late in the year, even if they sometimes came already in September. We spent far too much time first on negotiations and later on follow-up and explanations. All these problems were actually even more serious because we lived on such thin margins. Doing away with cost budgets did not mean less cost focus and fewer cost discussions. On the contrary, we probably had many more. But those discussions were much better and more relevant than the old budget discussions, and we had them all the time, not just once a year. It absolutely made sense to drop the budget, and it worked. Costs did not explode in Borealis, in fact they came down. This surprised even me, as I will discuss in more detail later.

But what if the situation is even more serious? Well, if I was running a company close to bankruptcy where you have to turn every penny every day, the last thing I would have done was to lock my spending for the next 12 months in a fixed and detailed cost budget.

Beyond Budgeting is *not* about ignoring the need for good cost management. On the contrary, a key objective is *better* cost management than what traditional budgets are able to deliver in today's business environment. In both the Borealis and Statoil cases I promise a lot of practical and hands-on advice on how to manage costs without budgets.

The Target-Setting and Evaluation Problem

Quality in performance evaluation starts with quality in target setting. Good targets are the foundation of any meaningful performance evaluation, and the two must therefore be addressed together. But even if we should get the target setting right, we often fail when we reach the performance evaluation. The classic mistake is to abdicate the right to apply any kind of assessment or common sense in the evaluation phase. We tie ourselves to the mast and leave it all to the numbers, reading the meter only, actual versus target. But no target is perfect and bulletproof. Unforeseen things happen and assumptions change. Blindly ignoring such realities does not make sense; changes must somehow be taken into account. The way targets are delivered is not irrelevant either. We therefore need a broader and more intelligent performance language than what the old language of "within budget" or "green key performance indicator" (KPI) represents. We discuss this topic in more detail at the end of this chapter.

Back to target setting and why we so often get it wrong here. A "budget" target is a predefined absolute number, a cost number, an income number, a production or market share number. The problem with such targets is their often narrow and misleading way of describing performance. Is it always good performance to hit the budget number? What if great value-creating opportunities were turned down because job number one was no budget overrun? Should we celebrate a project finished on cost and time, if quality took the backseat? What if value-adding scope changes were dropped because they would have meant cost or time overruns? Should we call for champagne when we hit the market share target, if two competitors unexpectedly went out of business and we had the market almost to ourselves?

Of course performance is about continuous improvement and about delivering on promises (defined the right way). But at the end of the day, performance is about outperforming peers; about being better than those you naturally can compare yourself with, inside or outside the company. No football team would define its main targets for the next season as scoring 45 goals or winning 50 points. (I am talking "European football" here!) In sports, it is all about beating the competition. Before the season, ambitions and targets set are about holding the fort or climbing in the league standings (or league tables as we would say in Europe). When measuring performance under way, it is very much about current position and trend on the same table. And when looking back at the end of the season in celebration or despair, it is all about where the team finally ended up. We should bring this sports thinking with us into our business lives. We should not blindly copy, but we should use more of it than we do today.

Although this is meant to be a "problem" chapter, let me also say a few words about possible solutions, because relative performance thinking is an important part of all the cases you will hear about later.

Benchmarking is nothing new in business. It has, however, mostly been used for sharing best practices, for learning and improving. That is a great purpose and something we absolutely shall continue doing. Yet there is an untapped potential in also using benchmarking more directly for *measuring and driving* performance, as a replacement for absolute targets, which typically get this job. These absolute targets tend to exist in parallel with the gentler best practice benchmarks, which is mainly conducted for learning purposes. We can do the learning purpose a big favor by lifting those benchmark tables into the strong spotlight that performance measurement enjoys in companies. There are important synergies in combining the two, because they reinforce each other.

League standings, internal or external, must of course consist of comparable teams that can learn from each other. League standings must also be based on relevant and meaningful performance metrics. Percentage ball possession or number of corners would not go down well as counting mechanisms in football. It is always debatable whether scoring more goals than the other team tells us who actually played best, but in this sport, it is agreed and accepted that this is how matches are won, 100% fair or not.

Beyond being a transparent performance measure, the league standing concept offers another major advantage. We can eliminate much of the target negotiation and the need for imposing targets from the top. This is important, because targets from above are never as motivating as those you set for yourself, based on external inspirations or on constructive challenges from above. The dilemma has been whether the sum of locally set targets will be ambitious enough when added together on a company level. But show me a manager or a team who is comfortable with lagging behind colleagues or competitors. How many will proudly declare "Below average is just fine with us"? This way of addressing performance reaches and pulls strings in teams and people that remain untouched in a traditional budget and target negotiation, where "everybody is negotiating to get the lowest number," as Jack Welch of General Electric put it.

Benchmarking is very much a *self-regulating* system, utilizing positive peer pressure to drive performance. It can simplify target setting drastically by setting such evergreen targets as "advancing in the standings," "being above average," and the like. It may even *remove* the need for targets. The purpose of a target is to get people to stretch and perform as well as they can. That is what a football team does, even if no specific league position is targeted. Again, nobody wants to be a laggard or to fall behind.

One of the less inspiring tasks in our company is monthly time recording. It is not a control mechanism but part of standard cost allocation mechanisms in the industry. It is easy to slip behind on this kind of duty. Some time ago the company issued benchmark data on missing hours across corporate staff units. There were no complaints, no order to improve, just the data. It did not take more than a month or two before a remarkable improvement had taken place in our time recording discipline.

There is, however, a possible and very serious negative side effect we must watch out for. As I just discussed, the purpose of comparing performance should not only be to get units to compete with each other. It is just as important that benchmarking stimulate sharing and learning from each other so that we lift the performance of the whole company. You want those sinking or those at the bottom to call those at the top and ask: "What are you guys doing so well that we obviously aren't?" But why should those at the top respond, when the caller ID shows that the laggard is calling again? It is nice to be up there among the best. Why would anyone want to undermine his or her own position by helping others lower in the standings?

This leads us to another key Beyond Budgeting issue, namely individual bonuses. Such bonuses discourage phones from being picked up. I have totally lost my belief in these types of bonus systems. A *collective* bonus is different, when, for instance, it is based on overall company performance against competition. That gives those on top a very good reason to pick up the phone or even start calling those below. We discuss this important topic in depth in the next section.

Relative targets can be very powerful, whether they are about connecting costs with output and deliveries or about comparing with others, or both. Yet it can be difficult to find relative performance indicators in all areas. We normally end up with at least some targets in the "absolute number" category, such as production, sales, cost, or market share. How do we evaluate performance against such targets, when the real world blows our assumptions to pieces like fragile palm trees in a tropical hurricane?

Just as we struggle with allocating cost budgets in an optimal way, we seldom have the insight of knowing *up front* which exact sales, production, or bottom-line number represents good performance and which does not. Of course we can have a view on what performance level we believe is required and what we aim to deliver, given certain assumptions. But what we really want is the best possible performance. Knowing up front exactly which absolute number this represents is seldom possible, unless we have been given some kind of divine insight into the future.

The answer lies in escaping the *mechanical evaluation* trap. When we evaluate performance against absolute targets, we must do more than just read the meter. We must *pressure test* the measured performance delivered. We need a quality assurance before we can conclude what kind of performance the actual outcome represents. There is so much relevant hindsight information available that is not there at target-setting time. Shall we, for instance, completely ignore the fact that someone had a massive tailwind that secured target delivery, while someone else had the opposite? Or that someone seriously violated company values in a blind chase for target delivery?

This kind of holistic hindsight evaluation must also be applied to relative targets. We will seldom or probably never find "perfect" metrics on which to build comparisons and league standings. Even a league standings position does not always reveal the full picture of the underlying performance.

What we talk about here is breaking the fixed and mechanical link between targets and performance evaluation. We can achieve this by using directional or relative targets where possible, but *always* combined with a holistic assessment where we appreciate and do not ignore hindsight information. Many people find this type of analysis more difficult than the mechanical way. It is more difficult, because it takes more leadership. The leader is hardly needed in the mechanical evaluation. A finance guy and a spreadsheet can do the job. I believe in simplicity, but not in this case. Leadership is not meant to be simple.

Let us close with a few final reflections on target setting. The first is about the SMART principles. These state that targets should be *s*pecific, *m*easurable, *a*chievable, *r*elevant, and *t*ime bound. It is a good test, but it easily can be misused in the hunt for the perfect target. Consider an example of a market share target. Should we set the target as % number or as a league standings position? Applying the SMART principles, the answer seems clear. There is no doubt that 17.2% is a more *specific*, or precise, target than "minimum number 2." But which one says more about performance? Is 20% great performance if those two competitors unexpectedly went out of business, and we could easily have been well above 25%? Precision does not always equal quality. The more accounting oriented we are in our performance thinking, the more we tend to emphasize precision and sacrifice relevance.

Target discussions are very often about data and numbers. Let us not forget that a target or a goal also can be expressed in *words*. A well-formulated goal or strategic objective can often motivate and drive performance better than cold numbers. The power of words should not be underestimated. Many people are more inspired by engaging and directional messages than by hard numbers. It is relevance versus precision again. We must, however, be careful with the detail level when we formulate "word" goals. Very specific and action-oriented ones can easily become the kind of straitjackets that budgets often are.

I can almost hear the reaction from some of my finance colleagues. "How on earth can we measure against something like that? It is only words!" Well, if that is what inspires people to do their best, what is most important: to get good performance, or to be able to measure exactly? Finance people should remember Albert Einstein's wise words: "Not everything that counts can be counted, and not everything that can be counted counts."

I recommend using the SMART principles with caution. Here is some advice to ensure that these principles actually help, not hinder, us in target setting.

- **S**pecific—but not a straitjacket
- **M**easurable—but do not forget words
- **A**chievable—but do not forget Aristotle
- **R**elevant—do not forget strategy and what we aim for
- **T**ime bound—do not leave it all for year-end

You will hear more about Aristotle later, who said: "Our problem is not that we aim too high and miss, but that we aim too low and hit."

The Bonus Problem

When I am presenting Beyond Budgeting in Europe, the first question I normally get is how costs can be managed without a budget. In the United States, the first question is often "What will drive my bonus if there is no budget?"

The smallest problem with individual bonuses is that they often are tied to delivery of budget numbers. Why this is not very smart has to do with how bad budget numbers often function as targets, as we discussed earlier. The other and much more serious problem with bonuses is their negative effect on motivation and performance, which this section is about.

I have already stated my position: I have totally lost my belief in individual bonus systems. I am convinced they do much more harm than good. But I have to admit I was once a believer. In my HR career, I was involved in both design and implementation of such systems. My skepticism has grown over time, and today my faith in them is gone. Again and again I have seen how not only do they fail to deliver what they promise, but also how much unintended damage they can cause. There are few areas with a bigger gap between what research says and what business does. Fifty years of studies almost unanimously discounts individual bonuses as an effective way of motivating and driving performance. Despite this, bonuses are alive and kicking; in fact, the trend is toward more bonuses, not less. But something is wrong. Satisfaction with the results cannot be what causes companies to change their bonus system, on average, every second year.

My views on this topic are rooted not only in the overwhelming number of supporting research conclusions. I have been on different individual bonus schemes myself since 1995. I know what makes me tick and what does not, and I do not think I am that different from most other people. At least that is what I hear when discussing with colleagues who are participating in the same bonus system. We all appreciate the money, but that is not what drives us.

Even if HR owns and operates this process in most companies, the economic theory that finance people (and most managers) subscribe to is where the problem starts. The assumption that has underpinned economic theory for a long time is the view of the human being as the rational, economic individual. Decisions and behavior are felt to be driven solely by optimization of one's own well-being and benefits, expressed and measured where possible in financial terms. The consequence of this assumption is that an employer-employee relationship becomes a "principal-agent" contract, where the main focus for both parties is to maximize one's own benefit. There is an assumed conflict of interest between the two, and the relation is reduced to a commercial transaction regulated in a detailed "performance contract" with an exchange of performance for money. If this is where we are coming from and what we believe in, then theory X and traditional management absolutely makes sense, including the bonus practices to be challenged in this section.

In my many meetings with management teams and employees, I often ask people their views on individual bonuses. I hear very much the same cynicism as I hear about budgets, not just from employees but also from managers. The vast majority of people do not like individual bonuses, do not believe they work, and can provide countless examples of how they lead to suboptimal behavior and have no or negative effects on motivation and performance. The paradox repeats itself: With so much dissatisfaction among people, where is the uproar, where is the revolution that we are starting to see on the budget side? I am, however, optimistic. I believe that one day individual bonuses will be driven out of town, shamed and undressed. But we need more little boys raising their hand, shouting what everyone in the crowd also can see: This emperor has no clothes on. Let me try to explain why he is naked.

The bonus system I am criticizing is the one that rewards individual performance for a limited group of executives and professionals, based on predefined targets. These targets are often budget or KPI numbers.

For more routine and transaction-oriented jobs, where the tasks themselves provide limited motivation, where individual results are easily measured, and where quantity is more important than quality, then individual bonuses might often work. What we are discussing here is something completely different; we are talking about leaders, professionals, and other knowledge workers charged with radically more challenging tasks and responsibilities, and where the link between individual effort and business results are far from mechanical and obvious.

Most companies have bonus systems for two quite different and unrelated reasons. The two are constantly mixed when the system is explained and justified. The first has to do with *market*, the second with *motivation*. The market reason is about recruiting and keeping good people. The argument is that the company needs to offer bonuses as a part of the total reward package in order to be competitive and attract and retain the people it wants to have onboard.

I can partly buy into this one. However, are we too quick in pulling the bonus lever? Are we creative enough in looking for alternative elements to put into our compensation offers? If it has to be money, does it have to be an individual bonus? Why does a collective system have no attraction power? Can sign-on fees sometimes be an alternative? Does it always have to be money? If we also include nonfinancial elements, the alternative menu available is even longer.

Are we underestimating the value of the company brand (assuming it is a good company we work for!)? The positive effect from employees proudly talking to friends and neighbors about how it feels to work with us can be extremely strong. When they talk about the opportunities and support they get, the right to raise their voice and also be heard, how they feel they make a difference, then they create a market pull much stronger than what any bonus system can provide. If, however, they share the very opposite messages, then no bonus system can fix it for us because the problems lie in a very different place. In the story about the Swedish Handelsbanken in Chapter 2, you will learn how this bank is able to attract great branch managers locally in the United Kingdom, even if the competition has massive individual bonus schemes and Handelsbanken has none.

My skepticism begins with the paradox that we recruit a person into what we proudly claim to be a knowledge organization boiling over with interesting tasks and challenges. We offer a fair base salary, but then add that "We really do not expect you to do your best. The tasks and the environment we can offer is probably not motivating enough. We will therefore put you on a bonus system. Only then do we expect you to go that extra mile." Unintentionally, this kind of message says quite a lot about the company and our new colleagues.

If the market argument does not come across convincingly enough, then "bonus believers" pull a very different argument out of their sleeves. Individual bonuses are great for motivation and performance! By tailoring the system the right way, we can almost program people into doing what we want them to do! We put a lot of effort into designing the nuts and bolts of the system. Which strings should we pull and how hard in order to make the marionettes dance as we want? Which targets? Which percentages? Which thresholds and ceilings? Which triggers and funding mechanisms? There is a whole consulting industry out there ready to help out on these questions. Coincidentally, there are some important issues these guys seldom bring up, because it might put them out of work. Those are the issues we will discuss here.

I am struck by how quickly we move to money as the lever to pull in order to motivate people. What happened to all those other levers we used to pull, before bonuses became the dominant one? It is almost as if we have given up on that old craft called leadership. Across cultures, research shows that autonomy, belonging, and mastering the job consistently is what people rate as most important. Money is way down the list.

Interestingly, respondents often believe that *other* people in the organization have money much higher up on the list than they themselves do. Autonomy, belonging, and mastering all have one thing in common: They require a much stronger leadership effort than dangling a financial carrot in front of people. Money is so much simpler. But again, leadership is not meant to be simple.

Bonus design work tends to focus entirely on the intended motivational effect on *those included* in the bonus system. A silent assumption is that there are no negative effects on those *not* included. Well, is that true? What about the guys just below? How motivating is it to work a certain body part off for your manager's bonus and get nothing yourself? The motivation effect is negative, not positive. Farther below the bonus borderline, the negative effect is probably smaller. It is more like an irritation, talked about around the lunch tables. People share stories and laugh about how senior managers pretend they are not acting in strange ways because of the bonus scheme. The negative effect on each person around the table is not that big, but the number of people being "only" irritated is huge, because they make up the rest of the organization. If we add up all these negative effects below the borderline and deduct these from the possible positive effect above, how much is really left? Is there anything left at all? Could it be negative? I hope you noted that I said "the *possible* positive effect," because I will challenge that assumption as well a bit later. Then the bonus problem becomes even worse.

Then there is the issue of *individual* bonuses. In the complex and interlinked reality in companies today, how individual is performance really? Isn't the Lone Ranger really something out of the past, riding into the sunset with a smoking gun after having solved the day's troubles completely alone? The large majority of us are highly dependent on others when doing our work and delivering on our goals, even when these goals have been set as individual ones. There is always some-one behind or next to us, contributing directly or indirectly to what we too often herald as individual success.

Next I would like to turn to another serious problem with individual bonuses. I did not want to start with this one, because it is the most difficult problem to get across. It goes straight for the throat of the motivation argument used by bonus believers. If you are among them, I needed to warm you up for this one. And just for the record, what you will hear is well documented in solid research and tons of studies, all quite easy to access.

A financial incentive is an external type of motivation; as psychologists would say, it is an artificial or *extrinsic* motiva-tion. It is a carrot hanging there to stretch and motivate people beyond what we believe the internal—or the natural or *intrin-sic motivation*—coming from the job itself is able to provide. It sounds quite logical; turbo-charge the intrinsic motivation by adding on external rewards. We get *more* motivation, right?

The problem is that research shows exactly the *opposite* effect; extrinsic motivation *reduces* intrinsic motivation. Please read that again. Extrinsic motivation *reduces* intrinsic motivation. Why this happens is still being debated. One explanation lies in what a bonus is all about: "Do this and get that." By introducing a bonus to get something done "more of" or "better," the focus naturally shifts from being just on the job or the task itself, to also what you get for it. The bonus *undermines* some of the interest in the job itself. Another related reason might be that bonuses *reduce* the value of the job and the tasks it pays for, even though the intention is the opposite. By offering bonuses, the message we send is that we do not believe you are sufficiently motivated by the intrinsic motivation coming from the job itself: solving problems, achieving goals, improving and innovating and everything else that has to do with thriving, blossoming, and growing both yourself and your job. All of this is obviously not enough. Carrots are needed in addition.

Giving blood is a great thing to do. Experiments have shown that when hospitals have increased the pay in order to get people to give more blood, the effect has been the opposite. Perhaps this is because most people feel that it reduces the noble act of giving blood to something closer to "selling body liquids," something you have to do for the money.

Even more disconcerting is what research says about work where a lot of *creativity* is involved or required. In such jobs, the negative effect of extrinsic motivation is even higher. This is bad news for most companies with individual bonus systems, because few would claim to have many jobs where no kind of innovation, creativity, and ability to think for yourself is required. This research finding becomes even more interesting if we think about *who* in companies are put on the bonus system. It is normally the higher management positions. Aren't these supposed to be among the most interesting and stimulating jobs there are in a company?

In his book, *Punished by Rewards*, social scientist Alfie Kohn tells a story about an old man who constantly is shouted at and insulted by a group of teenagers. One day he goes over to them and says, "I'll pay you a dollar for every insult you guys are able to come up with." The f-words immediately come flowing. The old man duly pays up, and asks the youngsters to come back the day after. "Then I will pay you 25 cents for the trouble." The boys show up and the insults again come strong and fast. The old man pays what he owes, but then tell them that from now on he will only pay them one cent per insult. "One cent!" the boys respond. "Forget it!" And they never come back.

Beyond illustrating how you can kill interest by rewarding people for something they used to do without a reward because they thought it was fun, the story also reminds us that incentives do not create any lasting and sustainable change in behavior unless you keep paying up. We should also remember that although a bonus is intended to be a positive reinforcement, it is just as much a punishment because it is also something that can be held back. The carrot is also a stick.

There are, however, a few camps in psychology that see things differently. The behaviorism theory of the famous American psychologist B. F. Skinner strongly advocates extrinsic motivation. The only small problem is that most of Skinner's supporting studies and experiments were conducted on mice, rats, and pigeons. The studies were about simple, mechanical, and repetitive tasks where individual results are easily measured—not exactly what life in today's knowledge organizations is about.

Kohn refers to more than 70 studies on people and organizations that all confirm the negative effects on motivation and performance. "This is one of the most thoroughly replicated findings in the field of social psychology," he says. "No controlled scientific study has ever found a long-term enhancement of the quality of work as a result of any reward system. For five years I have challenged defenders of incentive systems to provide an example to the contrary, and I have yet to hear of such a study," Kohn wrote in *Compensation & Benefits Review* in 1998. Still, this insight does not seem to have reached management theory, nor our HR functions. I find this very worrying. One reason why most managers and finance people are unaware of these findings might be that *any* knowledge and insight from psychology is met with suspicion and skepticism: "We are businesspeople, not shrinks!" *Leaders*, however, are more likely to be aware and understand what we just have talked about. HR, however, has no excuse for this ignorance or failure to act on this research.

You might, however, still be skeptical, so let me try another angle. A bonus system is a combination of *targets* and *rewards*, often introduced at the same time. When we claim that bonus systems work, which part is actually working? Could the real driver behind the observed effects actually be the increased effort we put into *communicating* around performance: direction, targets, progress, status, and next steps? Could it actually be all the increased attention that is delivering, not the bonus money? Some years ago a unit in Statoil introduced a local bonus system. This was a great success in terms of the performance improvement achieved, but the money involved was symbolic. The program worked, but obviously it was not because of the size of the bonuses offered.

What about other extrinsic motivation, like the public clap on the shoulder or a new exciting assignment? Although these examples are in the extrinsic category, research shows that positive feedback does not cannibalize intrinsic motivation in the same way as money does. Could this kind of motivation be more effective than we think? Are we simply throwing money out the window through our individual bonus systems?

Another serious side effect of bonus systems is so easily observed that I am amazed the bonus believers get away with it. It is the simple fact that bonuses drive people toward setting *lower* targets instead of the opposite, leading to lower performance and not higher, as is intended. Bonuses stimulate sandbagging, gaming, negotiation, and so much else that we hardly connect with a high-performing organization. Everybody knows this, even the bonus believers, even HR, but nobody reacts. It is a shame.

All the criticism so far has been directed at bonus systems designed as individual carrots. Team or collective bonuses are different, if they are designed more as a hindsight reward for shared success, in such a way that they encourage, not discourage, phones from being picked up. This is an important distinction. The individual bonus is intended to provide *both* up-front motivation as well as positive hindsight feedback. Collective bonuses are often criticized for not delivering that up-front motivation. But they are not meant to, for the reasons already discussed. Collective bonuses are mainly meant to create a positive feeling around common efforts and shared success being rewarded in a *fair* way. Creating such positive vibrations in the entire organization has, of course, a positive *indirect* motivational effect. Even if not everyone in the organization sees it like this, the possible negative motivational effect on these few people is small compared to the opposite positive effect on the large majority. With individual bonuses it is the other way around, to the extent that they produce any positive effects at all.

A frequently used argument against common bonuses where everyone is onboard is the "free rider," the person who never contributes but loves to share the prize. Free riders are real. They exist in every company and on many teams. But they still belong to a small minority. Again, we cannot organize our performance management around the minorities. We must use other mechanisms to deal with these guys.

If we really want money to do the job for us, with all problems we have just discussed, the bonus size and the prize at stake have to be so high, through increased bonuses and reduced base salaries, that it becomes a question of food on the table and a roof over the head. Beyond the moral aspects, such massive bonuses is about launching missiles where we abandon all control once the launch button has been pushed. We can only hope and pray that touchdown takes place as planned. Is this really something we want? Have we not seen enough examples of how terribly wrong this can go?

One additional argument sometimes comes up in my discussions with bonus believers when they realize that their other ones have failed to convince me. "We can save money. Bonuses are cheaper ways of paying people, because they are variable, not fixed." I do not buy this argument either. If we believe bonuses work, would we not actually want bonus costs as high as possible, because that reflects high performance?

Could it actually be that we pay *more* than necessary because it is actually not the money that works? Would it have been cheaper to revive that forgotten old craft called leadership instead? Remember autonomy, belonging, and competence?

If the cost argument holds, should we not get the same potential "savings" also with team bonuses? It will, anyhow, be a very costly saving if we also take into account all the negative consequences of individual bonuses just discussed. If affordability is the main issue, then a common profit sharing solves just that

It is interesting how bonus money somehow avoids any scrutiny when companies look to cut costs. How often do managers mention "reducing bonuses" when they are asked to come up with deep and radical cost-reducing actions? It is as if bonus money is some other kind of money, a very different currency protected by Harry Potter's invisibility cloak.

I accept that my views may be quite surprising if you have not heard individual bonuses being challenged before. If this is new for you, then you are not alone. The myths are strong and long-lived. If my arguments have not moved you, could we at least agree on one thing? Is it not fair to say that we at least need to *better understand* how the bonus system actually works in our own organization, because we spend quite a lot of money on it? Does it not make sense from time to time to check if the medicine is working? We should perform such a study ourselves, not hire management consultants, and we need to ask not just those who are in on the bonus system but also all those who are not. Perhaps we should do some research reading as well.

Let me close with a reflection on how the bonus area normally is organized in companies. This is not an attack on good friends working on the reward side, just something I find a bit strange. Usually the HR function is responsible for designing and operating the bonus system. Fair enough, but where in the HR function do we normally find this responsibility? It lies in the compensation and benefits department, together with pensions, employment contracts, union negotiations, and similar issues. We know why; bonuses are about money or variable pay. What is more logical than to place it with those responsible for all other compensation issues?

There is, however, an important difference between bonus and other pay issues. The smallest and simplest part of a bonus system is the compensation part, which is about market-relating payout levels. The complexity lies in designing what should *drive* the payout. This is a very different area. If the company is big enough to have a separate compensation and benefit unit within the HR function, there would normally also be a performance management unit or something similar in HR. *This* is where such an important topic belongs, because bonus is much more about motivational theory than it is about compensation. The compensation and benefit role in a bonus system should be limited to providing data on market levels. If this had been the case in more companies, I believe there would be far fewer individual bonus systems around. I actually sense much of the same skepticism in parts of HR as there is in the rest of the organization. There must of course be a close cooperation between these two HR units, but if there must be a bonus system, at least the responsibility should be moved.

Wherever the responsibility is placed, the big question remains. Why should we have individual bonuses at all? A survey by the major U.S. compensation and benefits consulting firm William M. Mercer sums it all up when concluding that "most merit or performance-based pay plans share two attributes; they absorb vast amounts of management time and resources, and they make everybody unhappy." Kohn recommends a simple way out of the misery: "Pay people fairly, and then do whatever possible to make them forget everything related to pay and money."

The Rhythm Problem

A very different type of problem in traditional management has to do with rhythm. As already discussed, business rhythm is uneven and unpredictable, and it is getting worse. Although we recognize the "global warming" effects, so far they have had few consequences for how we slice and structure our management practices. We still stick to a rhythm adopted from the fiscal year: January to December. We work harder and harder, trying to force the messy realities around us into the calendar year. It looks so logical and orderly in our schedules and flow charts. In reality, trying to adapt to the calendar year is more like forcing a wild tiger into a cage.

Just look at budgeting and planning. When finance people orchestrate this annual autumn ceremony, we tend to divide what is happening around us into three categories. In the first category we have the events that take place *before* the summer. These are OK. We would, of course, have preferred stability and as little new stuff as possible, because this makes planning even easier. But we accept that we live in a dynamic world. We have time to include these events in our instructions and budget assumptions and reflect them in next year's budget in an orderly way. We have control. So far so good!

Then we have all those events occurring *during* the budget and planning process. There can be many of these, given the increasing length of this process. We do not like these events very much. Shall we include them or not? Maybe we have to issue revised instructions and assumptions. They mess things up!

Finally, we have the stuff that strikes like lightning *just after* the budget is approved. Those events we simply hate. Why could not these things have happened earlier? Now our perfect budget is ruined, and our monthly deviation analyses next year will need to explain again and again that "This was not included in the budget." But we prefer it like this, at least compared to the unthinkable alternative of going back to the board with a new budget. We are professionals; we must demonstrate that we have control.

There is more we do not like in the real world. Projects and activities that run past year-end also mess things up. Even if a project stretching over several years is approved as a total at the project decision point, these long-term commitments often must be reapproved in each annual budget.

We see many of the same problems on the HR side. We organize almost everything around the calendar: annual goals, semiannual and annual performance reviews, manning budgets in the autumn, competence and deployment reviews in the spring. At the same time, in the real world, people change jobs all the time, projects and activities are assigned and completed as the business needs them, competence and resource gaps occur and are addressed continuously. Somehow we cope, but more *despite* than because of the calendar cycle.

Our forecasting rhythm is another example. It almost looks like driving a car with a very peculiar use of the car lights, the low beams for the short range and high beams for the long range. These lights help us see what lies ahead. We switch between the two in a fixed pattern that would create quite some attention in real traffic. During long autumn months we have the high beams on, not because it is a dark time of the year but because it is budget and planning time. They light up next year (budget) and also farther into the longer-term planning horizon. There is light all over the place. And of course a lot of light is needed to catch all the details we want to see. Then we turn the high beams off and start driving into next year with low beams only. At the beginning of the year, these lights illuminate all four quarters ahead. As we drive on and the quarters pass, the low beams gradually get covered with mud and become weaker and weaker, covering a shorter and shorter distance. But we do not mind, as long as we can see until year-end. Finally they cover only one quarter ahead, the fourth. Then we stop and clean the lights, so that we again can see farther ahead, into the whole of next year (budget time again!). We also turn the high beams on for a couple of months. And the pattern repeats itself.

Is this a safe way of driving in the dark? Why do almost all "business cars" use their lights in the same way, even if some travel on well-lit highways, others on dark and bumpy gravel roads, and some off-road in the wilderness where no car has driven before?

There might seem to be a very simple solution here: *rolling forecasts* that continuously look five or six quarters ahead. Is it really that simple? Is a rolling forecast not just another fixed and calendar-driven way of driving, still not recognizing the broad variety of roads business cars are traveling on? More about this in Chapter 4 on Statoil.

One reason for having lights all over the place is because we want to *coordinate*. We want to make sure that, once a year, projects are prioritized and scheduled, resources are matched with planned activities, and sales and purchases are coordinated and reconciled. We want everything to hang perfectly together, at least once a year. I have forgotten how many nights I have spent trying to reconcile internal services budgets because those idiots could not agree on how much one of them should to sell and the other one buy.

But why should everybody be coordinated around *one* cycle that feels like tomorrow for some and is beyond any reasonable planning horizon for others? How many can demand that their external customers already in the autumn commit to all orders for the whole of next year?

This is not an attack on coordination in general, only on the *annual* coordination stint. We need a coordination that is *continuous* and *customized*, where those who need to should communicate as they choose themselves, on a schedule and time horizon relevant for their business relation. This will seldom be once a year and for a January–December period. Coordination should also be very much about people meeting in networks and processes that run across the organizational structure, where direct contact between involved units at different levels is the norm that is encouraged and not blocked by the respective management layers above.

There are similar rhythm effects in other areas. Think about resource allocation, which is another purpose of budgeting (more about this and other purposes in the next section).

Steve Morlidge, who headed up Unilever's Beyond Budgeting project Dynamic Performance Management, has a wonderful metaphor on cost and capital budgeting. Imagine a bank telling its customers: "From now on, we are only open four weeks in the autumn. If you want to borrow money for a new car or for refurbishing your kitchen, you better be there in October. The rest of the year we are closed." That would be a pretty stupid thing for banks to say, and of course they do not.

But traditional budgeting by the book is very much like this. During "budget time" we have to identify all activities and resource needs for next year. Of course it is *possible* to ask for money also during the rest of the year. Yet just one look at the application process is enough to realize that this is not something the system encourages you to do. One of my old core competencies, in addition to explaining budget deviations, was to review such applications. We finance people both loved and hated this. We felt quite important when even senior managers had to submit written applications to us. But these reviews were a lot of work. Why had the managers not thought about this expense earlier and just put it in the budget? That would have been so much easier for all of us!

Business would come to a standstill if we actually followed the budget book by the letter. Fortunately, real life in companies is more flexible. There is a small back door into the bank that can be used the rest of the year. So what is the problem?

There are a few. First, the perception in the organization is often one of less flexibility than there actually might be. We have been quite successful in getting the message across: Budgets numbers are there to be met and not changed all the time. The consequence is that opportunities are lost or spending is suboptimized. People cannot find or do not want to knock on that back door.

Second, if we say that we are more flexible in practice, we are unclear in our communication. What actually are the rules of the game? Is it the strict process described in our budget procedures, or is it a somewhat more relaxed practice? Should we apply the same flexible approach in the ethics area as well?

It is not easy to force the real world into our well-organized processes. We are trying to make order out of chaos. We struggle and fail, year after year. Maybe the time has come to do the *opposite* and adapt our processes to the real world instead. Imagine if we started from scratch, with no baggage or historical constraints, and designed a process based on business rhythms. Would everything be squared into years, quarters, and months? Would everybody in the company be on the same rhythm? Would all targets have the same deadlines? Would all forecasting have the same time horizon? I doubt it. But we are on autopilot, stuck in historical traditions, comfortable with the convenience of doing things as we always have done them. "Change is good, but you go first" seems to be the mantra.

Let us hold that thought until we reach the Statoil case.

The Quality Problem

Most companies make budgets and business plans for at least three quite different purposes. They shall at the same time provide:

1. Good targets
2. Reliable forecasts
3. An effective resource allocation

All these three purposes are important elements in a good performance management model. What can be more efficient than having it all done in one go?

There are some serious problems involved in trying to do just that. These three purposes do not go well together. They are, in fact, very often in conflict with each other. Trying to force them into one process that produces "one number" often hurts the quality of all three purposes.

Take the forecasting purpose. A forecast should be our best guess on the future, the expected outcome, whether we like what we see or not. The purpose of a forecast is to get issues on the radar screen early enough to be able to take the necessary corrective actions. My experience is that when it is relevant and possible to make forecasts (which often is not the case!), people are reasonably good at doing so. They know their business and normally have a relatively good feel for which way the wind is blowing. They cannot make exact predictions but they can make good enough indications.

The budget and planning process is, however, not the place to hope for any high-quality forecasts. Let us take an example. Assume it is budget time again, and we are starting out with the forecasting purpose. We want to make a good sales forecast for next year. If we get this right, we have a good basis for also understanding expected production, manning, and cost levels. What happens, however, when we introduce one of the other purposes, like target setting? The minute a sales manager understands that the indicated sales forecast number will come back as a target, that number will start moving in a certain direction. Everybody wants to reach their targets, and everybody knows the consequences of missing out, whether they are on the bonus program or not.

The same happens on the cost side. If a sales or production manager is asked about the expected level of resources required for next year, and knows that the same number will become next year's cost budget, and also understands the consequences of a budget overrun . . . guess what?

By combining target setting or resource allocation as parallel purposes in a forecasting process, we pollute the quality of both the forecast and the other purposes. We should not blame the managers. Their response is both natural and predictable. We should blame our process, which puts people in difficult positions.

Another reason why we cannot combine targets and forecasts is because a good target needs to have an element of stretch and ambition. When setting targets, we cannot just sit in a dark room, or look back to last year and add on a few percentages. We need to look out the window to the world outside, to customers, shareholders, communities, and all the other external stakeholders, with expectations about our performance and behavior. While the window is open, it might be wise also to take a look at the competition and how fast it is running. When we close the window and reflect on what we have seen, it is not unlikely that what we have observed has an effect on our ambition level. Setting ambitious targets is less a decision we take and more a consequence of what is happening around us, whether we like what we see or not. At the same time, we need those good and reliable forecasts. We must understand where we are heading, how big the gaps are against our ambitions and targets, and where we need to focus our attention and energy to catch up. Forcing a target and a forecast into one number in one process is almost guaranteed to result in either a bad target or a bad forecast. Or very often both, since we negotiate and compromise and end up with a number somewhere in between.

By not clearly separating the two, we can forget about getting any early warnings in our budgets and business plans about possible gaps against targets. A forecast polluted by target setting or resource allocation cannot be trusted. These gaps do not disappear just because we do not see them. They just remain in the dark until it is too late to do something about them.

It is not possible to achieve any real quality improvement in target setting, forecasting, or resource allocation without first separating the three purposes. A two-step approach is needed: separate then improve. Going straight for the second step is guaranteed to fail.

The Efficiency Problem

It is an indisputable fact that we spend an enormous amount of time and resources on budgets and plans, first in making them and later when reporting against them. I have yet to meet anyone complaining about the opposite. According to the Hackett Group, companies spend on average 25.000 man-days on budgeting per billion USD in revenue.

I am addressing this problem last. Even if the figures are scary, it is still the smallest problem. Compared to most of the other problems, this is more like a mosquito bite: very visible but only irritating. It is not a mortal disease, just a very costly one. Still, this is where many companies believe they have their biggest problem, and therefore it is where many budget reengineering projects start.

Why do we spend so much time and energy on budgets and budget reporting? One reason is another of our traditional management myths: The more details and places of decimals we have in our plans and budgets, the more "control" we believe we have on the future. Or at least that is the impression we create, that these are "quality numbers." Isn't there something suspicious about people presenting a few rounded numbers only? Are these people just guessing? Have they done their homework?

There is no problem with details when describing where we have been and where we are. On the contrary, here they are needed and necessary to help us understand our business, the value and cost drivers and product and customer profitability.

The problem starts when we carry the same or almost the same level of detail with us into the future. The past does not carry uncertainty, but the future does. The farther ahead we look, the more uncertainty there is. This must have consequences for how detailed we try to describe the future. But the myth is strong: More details equal more quality. It does not look very professional or trustworthy to present expected sales or cost developments as a range with only a few numbers and a simple what-if analysis, although often this would be more "right" and certainly more honest.

It is amazing how blind people can become to the stupidity of fine-tuning, for instance, the expected USD exchange rate 10 years out in time, when doing it within the uncertainty span of what kind of superpower the United States will be by then. But somehow, working on those details seems to shield us and make all the big and scary uncertainties disappear.

My first budget process in Statoil in 1983 was a manual one, with roll after roll of paper consumed by our calculating machines as visible evidence of hard work and long nights. Today spreadsheets and software packages are an indispensable part of any budget process. But what happened to those promised

IT efficiency gains? Though I do not in any way miss the "manual" days, we have not utilized technology development to save
time but to crunch more numbers.

Since we are on this topic, I would like to share a little story
about my first encounter with the PC. The first one came to
Statoil late 1983, to the planning department, which of course
was separate from the budget department where I was based.
It took the planning guys half a year to convince their boss to
make this $8,000 investment. It was probably not in their budget.
The second PC landed with us budget guys a few months later.
It was a very early IBM model, with a double floppy disk station
and no hard disk. Those floppy disks were just that, very floppy.
We carried them like diamonds to avoid any damage. Saving and
backup was a slow and time-consuming effort, but we learned
our lesson after having lost our work for the third time because
the cleaning lady pulled the plug to fire up her vacuum cleaner.
"How should I know there are people in the office this late at
night?"

The PC was located in a common area for everybody to
use. The first couple of weeks a few colleagues and I had it
almost for ourselves. Then the interest picked up, and we had
to put up a booking list. I spent several months transferring
a range of manual tasks into SuperCalc spreadsheets (anyone
remembering SuperCalc?). Then I started to harvest from my in-
tensive investment. Apart from the cleaning lady, it was a great
experience—at least for a couple of months. Then a colleague
came over, telling me that he had some good but also some
bad news. "There is a new and much better spreadsheet coming, called Lotus 1-2-3. Unfortunately, it's not compatible with
SuperCalc." I spent the next months redoing all my work. For
a few years I was actually one of the company spreadsheet ex-
perts. I left that role many years ago, with no regrets. Today, my
younger colleagues smile when I ask them for help on those
rare occasions when I open Excel.

But back to budgets. Another fascinating phenomenon in the annual budget game is the "elevator rides." The bigger the company, the funnier (or more tragic) it is. It starts early, with the initial data production in the front line. The numbers are then consolidated, level by level, week after week, until they one day reach top management. For corporate budget and planning people, this is an important moment. The suit and tie is put on, and the ceremony starts. After the CEO has thanked everyone for all the hard work through long nights and weekends, the message comes: "Is this really the best we can do? I had expected higher sales, lower costs, more of this, less of that. I want you back next week with better numbers."

And then the numbers are sent down the elevator again. At the lower floors, people are almost waiting at the sliding doors. Everybody knows they are coming and what the message is. And everybody is well prepared. Of course there is something to give, on costs, on manning, on sales budgets. Some of the fat is sliced off, ambitions are increased, but only a bit. And up again the numbers goes. This time the atmosphere is slightly more positive. "Great work, but is this *really* the best we can do?" And down again they come . . .

I would not be surprised if we talk about three to four elevator round trips in larger companies. But everybody is happy: top management, because they believe they have stretched the organization to the limit; people in the organization, because they got away with it this year as well.

We might smile about all of this, as we picture Dilbert on his way up the elevator. But it is not very funny. How many customers out there are really willing to pay us for spending time on such stupidity? Is there a better example of a non–value-adding activity, even before we include the negative effects on morale and motivation?

But the resource waste does not stop here. Now comes all the reporting against budgets. Monthly detailed deviation analyses explain down to the last penny where and why we are off track. This is a core competence with many finance people. I have been there too. I once kept track of different types of deviation analyses produced during the year. On a top-10 list, there was one explanation coming out on top, year after year. Can you imagine which one? It was: "The monthly distribution in the budget is wrong." What a deep and insightful analysis from a highly paid finance guy! A great piece of advice to help a management team get back on track!

By the way, consider a bit the word "deviation." It is a negative word, something unwanted. Something else happened compared to what we had planned, and we do not like it. The real world has taken a different route. A more natural word would be "variance," but that is probably not negative enough.

CHAPTER 2

Beyond Budgeting

Beyond Budgeting Round Table

One day in 1996, shortly into the Borealis journey, I noted a small ad in the UK *People Magazine*. An organization called CAM-I (Consortium of Advanced Management, International) wanted to contact companies exploring alternatives to budgeting. I called the listed number and got Jeremy Hope on the phone.

That was my first contact with Jeremy, and soon also with Robin Fraser, who together wrote the book *Beyond Budgeting* some years later. We had a long talk and later met several times as they wrote two case studies on Borealis.

Jeremy and Robin got positive responses from several other companies, and in 1997 they established the Beyond Budgeting Round Table (BBRT), with close to 40 companies joining in from the start. Today there are more than 100. The round table is a member-driven meeting place for both companies and public organizations, where participants share their own experiences and learn from each other through case studies, presentations, and discussions. A great advantage compared to the conference circuit is the high trust level among members and the open sharing of both successes and failures. Member companies range from small to large, from those just interested, to those having started on the journey. They all have one thing in common: They realize that something is wrong with traditional management and want to do something about it.

BBRT today has a global reach, with round tables in Europe, the United States, the Middle East, and Australia. In Europe, a dedicated forum for German-speaking companies has also been set up. I am currently the chairman of the European BBRT.

For me, BBRT has been an invaluable source of knowledge and inspiration, providing new perspectives and new destinations. Jeremy Hope, Robin Fraser, Steve Morlidge, Peter Bunce, Franz Röösli, and Steve Player have all been great sparring partners and challengers on the journey.

I recommend a visit to the round table at www.bbrt.org, and also Hope and Fraser's book, *Beyond Budgeting: How Managers Can Break Free from the Annual Performance Trap* (Harvard Business School Press, 2003).

The Beyond Budgeting Concept

The early observations and first attempts in the BBRT to formulate concepts and models started where most companies also start: with the more concrete and obvious problems with budgeting. Research and new cases gradually led to an understanding that the budget problem was just one part of a larger *systemic* problem. The solution could therefore not be found just in new *tools* and *processes* that could do the budget job in a better and more effective way. A new set of *leadership principles* was also needed. Together, these form a coherent model, consisting of six leadership principles and six process principles. You will recall many of the themes that we discussed in Chapter 1. Most of the recommended solutions will occur in the case stories later on. Here are the 12 principles.

Leadership Principles

1. **Customers.** Focus everyone on improving customer outcomes, *not on hierarchical relationships*.
2. **Organization.** Organize as a network of lean, accountable teams, *not around centralized functions*.
3. **Responsibility.** Enable everyone to act and think like a leader, *not merely follow the plan*.
4. **Autonomy.** Give teams the freedom and capability to act; *do not micromanage them*.
5. **Values.** Govern through a few clear values, goals, and boundaries, *not detailed rules and budgets*.
6. **Transparency.** Promote open information for self-management; *do not restrict it hierarchically*.

Process Principles

7. **Goals.** Set relative goals for continuous improvement; *do not negotiate fixed performance contracts*.
8. **Rewards.** Reward shared success based on relative performance, *not on meeting fixed targets*.
9. **Planning.** Make planning a continuous and inclusive process, *not a top-down annual event*.
10. **Controls.** Base controls on relative indicators and trends, *not on variances against plan*.
11. **Resources.** Make resources available as needed, *not through annual budget allocations*.
12. **Coordination.** Coordinate interactions dynamically, *not through annual planning cycles*.

It is important to understand how the two sets of principles support each other in a holistic model and how they depend on each other. Process drives behavior, and vice versa. The way we set up our management processes must support and drive the leadership behaviors we want to see.

Many people ask how critical it is to fully implement all 12 principles. The question is relevant, because there is a mouthful in each of them, as they each represent a change project in itself. Being on a Beyond Budgeting journey can sometimes feel like eating an elephant. There is just one way to do that; it must be sliced up in smaller parts. The different parts do not make up a buffet menu where we can pick a few here and there and hope for any real change. At the same time, the relative importance of each principle might vary depending on the business in question. This is not fast food, but as in real life, the results are also much healthier.

Beyond Budgeting is less of a recipe and more of a philosophy, supported by these guiding principles. It is more of a journey than it is buying an instant new management box. That is why solutions may vary somewhat from company to company. One thing is, however, nonnegotiable: The journey must address both the leadership and the process side. The right timing and order might vary; this will be discussed further in Chapter 5 on implementation.

Many people are frustrated because Beyond Budgeting does not come as a box with a simple instruction manual. In Statoil, a system documents all major processes through flowcharts. I once was asked to draw Beyond Budgeting as such a process. It cannot be done, at least not more than a small part. When I was a boy, I complained to my first math teacher how difficult it all was. "It is not meant to be simple" was her answer. The same goes for Beyond Budgeting. Although it is all common sense, it is not meant to be simple.

The Handelsbanken Case

The most famous Beyond Budgeting case is the Swedish Handelsbanken. What makes the story so fascinating is not just the fact that the bank decided to completely change its management model all the way back in 1970 and has stuck to it since. Equally important is how it has performed. The bank has consistently been more profitable than the average of competitors *every* year since 1972. Its cost performance is just as impressive. The bank is among the most cost efficient not just in Scandinavia but also globally, a position achieved without cost budgets. All those other banks with higher costs will most likely claim that their costs would increase even more if they took away the cost budget.

Many case studies have been written about Handelsbanken. I will therefore limit myself to a short description of the main principles in its model. The wise and brave man behind this radical move was Jan Wallander, chief executive of Handelsbanken from 1970 to 1978 and later chairman of the board until 1991.

When he joined the bank in 1970, he decided to completely change the leadership and management model. Handelsbanken had until then been managed more or less like other Swedish banks, with very much the same mixed results. Wallander's vision was a radically decentralized model. He wanted to replace traditional management controls like budgets, hierarchy, centralization, secrecy, and individual rewards with completely different "controls." He strongly believed a new model would stimulate and drive good performance much more effectively, and deliver what he did *not* regard as two conflicting purposes: high customer satisfaction and low cost. These bold steps included:

- Much greater branch and regional authority
- A flat structure, with a few layers only
- A focus on customers instead of products
- Transparent performance data
- No individual bonuses, only a collective profit-sharing system

- A strong value-based culture
- No budgets

Many people see eliminating budgets as Wallander's main and bravest decision, but this was just as much a natural consequence of the new model as a goal in itself.

The explanation behind the bank's remarkable success lies of course very much in what it started doing but also in everything it stopped doing. It did not just put one new box on top of the ones it already had. Handelsbanken is thin on traditional management processes but strong on direction and values and on freedom and flexibility. It does very little target setting and very little traditional planning. Its model can be summarized in this way:

- Drive performance and learning through transparent internal benchmarking between regions and branch offices.
- Provide sufficient freedom and responsibility to enable each branch and region to do what is right to lift its own performance.
- Balance the individual drive with a shared purpose through a common bonus scheme for all employees, and no individual bonuses.

Each month, the head office in Stockholm issues a report on a few selected key performance indicators that describe the performance of regions and business areas. These indicators are not perfect but are accepted throughout the bank as good enough. They include return on capital and cost/income ratio. The regional head offices issue similar reports covering the branch offices within each region.

This is all that Stockholm does. For those whose internal rankings are low or sinking, there are no additional instructions from above about increasing sales, cutting costs, more of this, less of that. The message from the head office lies in the comparison with others: "We can see that you are struggling. You are, however, closest to the market, you are closest to the customers, and you know your people best. "We are more than happy to help out if you want us to, but your performance is your responsibility." Within a few boundaries, branches have the necessary authority to take action as required. This includes not only wide lending authorities and all marketing activities (the bank runs almost no central marketing campaigns) but also the full cost side, including recruitment and salary levels. One expression in the bank is that "Our chairs have no backs to lean on." If you make the wrong move, there are no head office instructions to blame.

But who is comfortable with falling behind? Those at the bottom work hard to improve, those at the top work hard to keep their position. Everybody tries to improve. Those at the top also have an incentive to help those below, because there are no individual bonuses involved (except in a small trading environment at group headquarters). Profit sharing is collective and driven by another ranking: how the bank performs against other banks. Everyone is onboard, not just with the same percentage, but even with the same amount. The annual bonus is not paid out but invested in an inhouse fund called Oktogonen. This fund invests the bonus payout, some of it in Handelsbanken shares, where today it owns around 10% of the bank. An individual's share is paid out only at retirement or when he or she leaves the bank. There are no short-term carrots dangling. If you had been with the bank since 1972, when the scheme was established, your balance today would be around €800,000.

With no individual bonuses, how is the bank able to attract and retain good people in a business where bonuses are standard, at least on manager level? In the United Kingdom, where Handelsbanken is expanding rapidly, recruiting new branch managers is not a problem. "Actually, they call us, because they want to work for us," says Magnus Uggla, head of

Regional Bank South. "They have heard about us, and they like our philosophy and the way we work. We don't have to offer individual bonuses; our model is obviously attraction enough." He also explains that when opening a new branch, they first recruit the branch manager, and then move on with the rest, not the other way around.

Jan Wallander's job experience prior to joining the bank in 1970 included public sector forecasting. This was probably why he arrived at his very logical but still unique view on forecasting. He writes in his book *The Budget: An Unnecessary Evil* about all the efforts put into forecasting sales of TV sets in Sweden and how they got it wrong again and again. When he moved to the bank, he decided not to try even harder to forecast but rather the opposite. If things are stable and you believe tomorrow will be like today, why *should* you spend time on forecasting? You know what tomorrow will look like. And opposite is true as well; if times are turbulent and you have no idea what tomorrow will be like, how *could* you spend time on forecasting? You are most likely wrong anyway.

Hearing and reading about how a company operates is one thing. Talking to people, especially on the front line, sometimes can reveal a different picture. I have met and discussed the actual practices in Handelsbanken with a number of people in the organization. The story they all tell is very consistent. They describe the same philosophy and the same practices. One former branch manager turned out to be someone I studied with. We met each other on a plane some time ago. When exchanging career updates, he mentioned that he once had been responsible for starting up a new Handelsbanken branch in Norway. I immediately used the opportunity to test out the general case. Without any leading questions from my side, he confirmed everything I had heard already. The freedom they had, the power of the internal benchmarking and all the other elements of the model.

Some people wonder if the Handelsbanken model means a soft approach, with middle and top management shying away from tough decisions, with a hands-off approach to difficult issues. Let there be no doubt: Difficult issues *are* being handled. But they are being handled where they actually exist. The majority of such cases always will be on the front line, often related to customers or employees. One local branch manager explained how he had replaced more than half the team when he started "because they were not good enough in their current roles." He did not do this because he was told to but because he had to, in order to lift the performance of the branch. It should also be mentioned that those people went to other and more suitable jobs elsewhere in the bank. The bank has a long-term view not only on customer relationships but also on employment. It does not fire its employees.

Handelsbanken is a fascinating case, for many reasons: its radical but simple model, how long it has stuck to the same philosophy, and its consistently high performance. I have often wondered why competitors are not trying to copy Handelsbanken. There are no secrets. The entire model is visible, with no copyrights. Perhaps it does not come across as advanced enough. Or maybe the other banks actually understand that this is a long journey and not a quick fix that will provide results tomorrow. Perhaps they lack the energy to get started or realize they do not have the patience to follow it through, or is the love of and addiction to power and authority simply too strong? It reminds me of Toyota and U.S. car manufacturers—although the Americans seem more interested in Toyota than the bank business seems to be in Handelsbanken.

It is a long journey, but the earlier you start, the farther ahead of the competition you will be. It takes just as long for them; one day they will wake up and realize that this is something they simply *have* to do, whether they want it or not. And the longer journey that creates real and sustainable change is far better than quick fixes that only scratch the surface and leave no permanent marks.

For those of us working in other businesses, there is still a lot to learn from the Handelsbanken case. I disagree with those saying that because units in their business are not as comparable as bank branches and regions, there is little to learn. The Handelsbanken model is about much more than peer groups and benchmarking. It is about trust, transparency, and simplicity. The benchmarking just makes it a bit easier.

CHAPTER 3

The Borealis Case

Introduction

You have now heard about the many problems caused by traditional management practices, where budgets and the budgeting mind-set play a major role. I hope those first chapters made you realize the seriousness of the problem we are up against and its systemic nature. We have been through the Beyond Budgeting philosophy and main principles of the model, and we have briefly looked at Handelsbanken as a great example of the model applied in practice. I hope you now want to hear even more about different ways of getting out of the misery.

We will now move to the two cases I know best, Borealis and Statoil, as I was responsible for both. Neither case should be taken as mechanical recipes. They are both rooted in the specific business, culture, and situation of each company. Nevertheless, I believe they offer quite a range of advice relevant for your own organization. Feel free to borrow and copy. There are no secrets and no copyrights here.

As you will learn, neither of the two could be called full-fledged Beyond Budgeting cases, as defined by the 12 Beyond Budgeting principles. Together, however, they do provide a good illustration of what a Beyond Budgeting journey is all about. Borealis was an early case, primarily focused on finding new and better tools to replace the budget. This was also where the Statoil case started, but it has evolved into questioning and addressing also bigger leadership issues.

Creation of Borealis

In the early 1990s, both Statoil and the Finnish competitor Neste were struggling with their petrochemical businesses. Statoil's petrochemical business was small on a European scale. Even after acquisitions in Belgium, Sweden, and Germany, lack of size was a major competitive disadvantage. Neste's petrochemical division had been in a similar situation, which had triggered an aggressive international expansion strategy. Within a short time Neste had acquired new capacity in several European countries, on a much larger scale than Statoil.

The petrochemicals business is extremely cyclical, with great peaks and serious downturns as a repeating pattern. The raw materials for this industry are petroleum based (naphtha, propane, butane, etc.); therefore, they have much of the price volatility of oil. Its products, various plastic raw materials, go into both consumer and industry segments where demand and prices typically are driven by other factors, at least short term. Being caught between such relatively unrelated markets has always been a major challenge for the industry.

The early 1990s was no exception. This time the market was down, after a period of solid margins. In Neste, the result was a serious cash squeeze, because the company had severely stretched its financial muscles through the international expansion. For Statoil, the situation was quite different. The company was financially solid. The petrochemical business also served as a hedge for the oil- and gas-producing part of the company. But size was still an issue. Guess what happened.

The merger was announced late 1993, and the new company started up in March 1994. The company was named Borealis, after the northern light phenomenon aurora borealis, honoring its Nordic roots. It became Europe's largest petrochemicals company, with 5 major sites and some 30 plants spread across Europe, from Finland to Portugal. To the surprise of many, headquarters was located in Copenhagen, Denmark—"neutral" territory for both companies, with competitive business terms and a practical location with direct flight connections to all sites. Equally important, the country has a lot of bright people. This became a real asset for Borealis when expatriates from all over Europe joined forces with new Danish colleagues.

I came from a job as finance manager for Statoil's oil marketing and trading unit. In late 1993, I started my petrochemicals career as head of Corporate Control in Borealis, responsible for financial control, accounting, and tax. Yes, I did pick that name myself!

It was a great time, in a great company. There was a pioneer spirit flowing through the organization, inspired by the first of the four Borealis core values: "One company—new, different and better." It was a new start in many ways. To ensure we wore only one hat in the new company, members of the new management team had to resign from their respective mother companies. We were even told to buy, not rent, accommodations in Copenhagen, to demonstrate a firm and long-term commitment to the new company. None of this created much discussion. The enthusiasm was strong and real.

The Journey Begins

The company started operations in March 1994. It did not take long before the issue of budgets came up. "We need a budget for 1994!" Never mind that almost half the year had passed before it was finished. It was a tough job. We had limited historical data on the new company. Many were new in their positions, preparing budgets in parallel with a lot of integration tasks. We were all pretty exhausted, but there was little time to rest. Next year was approaching fast. Once we completed the 1994 budget, we immediately started preparing the 1995 budget.

When we finally could sign off the second budget made that year, we decided to direct the minimal energy we had left into a "lessons learned" workshop. Our minds were set on "continuous improvement," and we spent the day discussing peanut issues. Should we ask for this number instead of that number? Should we add a column here and delete a column there? Really important stuff!

There was one guy in particular who was completely knack-ered that day. Normally an active person with many constructive ideas, the site controller from Norway was suspiciously quiet. Then suddenly, out of nowhere, looking up at the ceiling, he said: "What if we don't budget at all?" We all looked at him, and we all probably thought the same thing: This guy needs a holiday. And that was it. We shrugged it off and finished the meeting, after having agreed on some completely unimportant improvements to the Borealis budgeting process.

A few months went by. The integration had gone well and spirits were high, even if the business was up for a rough ride again with rapidly declining margins. This also meant that our price and margin assumptions in the 1995 budget were completely wrong, just as they had been in the 1994 bud-get. Everything that built on these assumptions was now quite useless for us, and the year had hardly begun. But the bud-get was still our reference point, requiring long analyses each month explaining why we were off track. But at least we could explain...

By now it had become clear to the new management team that merger synergies were not enough. A radical overhaul of all operating processes was required to avoid falling behind and to prepare for a future where everybody expected average margins to continue their merciless downward slide.

This led to the birth of "Value for Money," a large business reengineering project. The consulting company Gemini was called in to support. The message was simple: Leave no stone unturned and look for a better way. The consultants were bright guys, although I was taken aback by the many young faces with rather soft skin on their hands. Young or more experienced, challenging the budget was not part of their vocabulary.

I was asked to head up a part of the program called "Management Effectiveness." This cryptic title led to my simple question to the chief financial officer, Svein Rennemo: "What do you expect?" You will recall his response: "I expect the unexpected." Backed with such a mind-blowing mandate, we went to the task really fired up, wanting to make a difference. The whole company was in change mode. Other functions and units went to work on their own processes, but no one had the kind of mandate we had received.

It did not take long before that crazy comment from a few months earlier came back to us: "What if we don't budget at all?" Of course we knew the budget process was flawed. That was an old insight, not just from the two budgets we made the year before but from many years of previous budgeting experience in the team. "This is it!" we said. "Let's blow up the budget!"

We immediately went back to Svein, glowing with excitement as we shared with him what we wanted to do. When the obvious question came about what would replace the budget, we had to admit that we had no clue, not yet. "Maybe you should go and find out" was his short and simple response, again with that little smile on his face.

It would take quite some time before we could answer his question. We moved on by spelling out more clearly what wanted to achieve. That list was short on words but high on ambitions, as shown in Exhibit 3.1.

◤ BOREALIS _____

Why shall we abolish traditional budgeting?

We want to:

- Improve our financial management and performance measurement

- Decentralize authority and decisions

- Simplify the process and reduce time spent

_____

EXHIBIT 3.1 The Vision

Shortly after, we spotted an article in a Swedish magazine. The title read "Volvo drops budgeting." Wow! There *is* actually someone trying this! This was before the days of the Beyond Budgeting Round Table (BBRT), with no conferences to attend and no books on the topic as far as we knew. We were actually far down the road before we heard about Handelsbanken, even if the bank already had been operating without budgets for 25 years, and only some 100 miles away!

We immediately went to visit Volvo, and came back with some new insights but also somewhat confused and uncertain about how much the company really had done. But inspiration hit again when somebody showed us the famous Jack Welch quote: "Budgets are the bane of corporate America!" If *he* could say this, we must be on to something!

With no solution or alternative in sight, we continued with describing what we saw as the problems with traditional budgeting. That was not a difficult job. The issues came pouring out of the project team, and very soon the list looked like Exhibit 3.2.

Actually, the initial list looked *almost* like Exhibit 3.2. The first point about conflicting purposes only came to us a month or two later. That insight turned out to be key to finally discover the alternatives to the Borealis budget.

BOREALIS

Traditional budgeting has many weaknesses....

- Conflicting purposes—target setting versus financial forecasting

- Not only a ceiling—also a floor for costs

- Promotes centralization of decisions and responsibility

- Inflexible to changes in planning assumptions

- Tends to make financial control an annual autumn event

- Absorbs significant resources across the organization

EXHIBIT 3.2 The Case for Change

The period before we arrived at that understanding was a time when our enthusiasm started to fade and was gradually replaced with a feeling of resignation and failure. We *knew* the process was flawed, that was not the issue. But how could we find this one single great tool that could replace the budget and solve all our problems? Had we been too arrogant when we declared war on the budget?

We discussed, we read, and we searched. And "searched" meant something else in 1995 than it does today. There was no Internet and no Google there to help us. The writing was on the wall. We could not find anything. Svein Rennemo's great mandate did not sound that great anymore. For a few weeks we were close to giving up.

But then we finally asked ourselves a very simple question: *Why do we budget?* What is it we actually use the budget for? What are the different purposes? This was not exactly a rocket science question, but we simply had not thought about it from that angle before. It was another magic moment. Just like pushing a button, answers came pouring out. Within half an hour we had our first list of different budget purposes. With the list on paper, it soon became clear that many of these purposes were not that closely related. A few were even in conflict with each other. We also realized that the answer did not lie in that one great new tool we had been dreaming about. Instead, we understood that we had to look for a set of *tailored* tools and processes, each one dedicated to one of the different budget purposes.

We went on to define and design these individual tools, purpose by purpose. This was yet another great exercise. The new tools and solutions suddenly became blindingly obvious for us: rolling forecasts, balanced scorecards, activity account-ing, trend reporting, decision authorities, and so on. No rocket science! For a minute, we were almost disappointed. Could it really be this simple? We later learned that it was not. The challenge was not to find and implement these new tools; it was to demolish the old budget mind-set in people's heads and replace it with a very different kind of leadership and behavior.

It also became clear that one of these new tools already was under development right under our noses, the balanced scorecard. We decided to use the scorecard for target setting and performance monitoring. Other tools needed to be designed and built, but at this stage we could already see quite clearly how the tools would work and how the whole process would fit together.

Then our next picture was ready. We knew not only what we wanted to achieve and what the problems were, but also what would replace the budget. (See Exhibit 3.3.)

All illustrations in this chapter are, by the way, "originals" from the Borealis days. These are the pictures we used to ex-plain the model to the organization and later to the outside world.

BOREALIS

We can achieve what the budget does in a better way

The budget was used for:	We achieve the same through:
• High-level financial and tax planning	✓ Quarterly rolling financial forecasts
• Target setting	✓ Targets on the balanced scorecard
• Controlling fixed costs	✓ Trend reporting ✓ Cost targets where and when needed ✓ Activity approach
• Prioritizing and allocating investment/project resources	✓ Small projects—trend reporting ✓ Medium projects—varying hurdle rates ✓ Major strategic projects—case by case, the budget was never a tool
• Delegation of authority	✓ Use existing mandates/authority schedules

EXHIBIT 3.3 The Budget Alternatives

The Borealis Model

Let us take a closer look at the different elements in the new model. First, I want to remind you that the Borealis case was mainly an attempt to solve the more tangible in-your-face problems with budgeting. I am still proud of our courage and what we achieved. But I do not think any of us at the time fully understood how all of this fit in a larger organizational context, as building blocks in an alternative leadership model. Personally, this was before my days in human resources (HR) and before long hours of discussions with friends in the BBRT and good colleagues in Statoil.

However, the project was not only about tools. We clearly sensed that there was something more to what were embarking on. It was no coincidence that our second purpose read "Decentralize decisions and authority."

The reaction in the company was much more positive than I had expected. I do not think too many fully understood where we were heading, or all the new tools, but we got a lot of positive feedback just for *daring* to attack the "budget monster." It also helped that the company was in change mode. All over the place, the mantra was "New, different, and better." I have never experienced a value statement being so powerful, giving people so much direction and energy.

Exhibit 3.4 shows the way we explained how the new processes would not only cover what the budget had done for us but also give us a lot more. "More for less" was an expression we often used. Again, Svein Rennemo was gently pushing us: "We need *one* simple picture that summarizes what this is all about." (See Exhibit 3.4.)

 **BOREALIS**

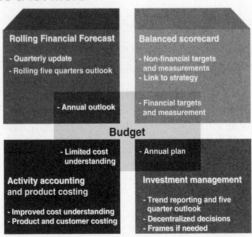

EXHIBIT 3.4 More for Less—The New Model in a Nutshell

Five-Quarter Rolling Forecasts

"For high-level financial and tax planning, we need reliable financial forecasts. These do not require a lot of details on cost, because the purpose is not cost management. And why should a forecast stop at year-end? This is not an accounting exercise. A continuous five-quarter horizon in our business makes sense," we concluded in one of our project meetings. That was it! The Borealis rolling financial forecast was born.

We had a mental picture of what the new forecasting process should look like. It should be so simple that we could write it out on the back of an envelope. Although we ended up using a few more envelopes and a simple spreadsheet, it still was a very lean process, where quality meant "roughly right." If we got it wrong, it only lasted a quarter anyway, then we made a new forecast.

Another reason for choosing a five-quarter horizon was the Borealis owners. Both Statoil and Neste had traditional budgets and needed budget numbers from us. With a five-quarter horizon, we could use the forecast we made in the autumn as the budget they requested. Our horizon then covered the last quarter and the next calendar year. We carved out next year, renamed it "budget," and shipped it off. Fortunately, both owners were reasonable in their follow-up and did not demand too much reporting against these numbers. They were happy and we were happy.

Today, the five-quarter rolling forecast has almost become a standard in Beyond Budgeting implementations. Some people even believe that Beyond Budgeting equals rolling forecasting. That is one of the most common misunderstandings about the concept. In Statoil, we did not implement a five-quarter rolling forecast. I will explain why not and what we are considering instead in Chapter 4.

Balanced Scorecard

One of the new tools came to us through a recommendation from Gemini Consulting. The "balanced scorecard" was a new concept introduced by Robert Kaplan and David Norton in an article in *Harvard Business Review* in 1992 titled "The Balanced Scorecard: Measures That Drive Performance."

I assume you are reasonably familiar with the balanced scorecard concept, so I will not explain it further. If not, I recommend one or more of the Kaplan and Norton books. None of these books was available in 1992; the article was our only theoretical guidance beyond the consulting support we got. Gemini did not have much to offer on the topic, so it subcontracted the consulting company Renaissance for the job. We found the article and the thinking behind very fascinating. We were especially intrigued by the key performance indicators (KPIs). Finally, we would get the full and complete insight into all the different drivers behind our business results. It felt like the Holy Grail was buried just around the corner. We did not yet, however, see the relevance of the balanced scorecard for the other and, for us, much bigger question: What could replace budgets?

A scorecard project group was established. The executive committee was very enthusiastic and heavily involved. There was a textbook start, with several long workshops with this key group of people. Design of the first Borealis scorecard proceeded well. The only problem was that it turned out to be more difficult than we had expected. Looking back, we clearly searched too hard for the perfect scorecard and sacrificed too much simplicity and clarity on the way. We started out with scorecards at the group and business unit level. Some business units decided to go farther down to plant level.

Then came the day when we cracked the issue of the different budget purposes. As you will recall, target setting was one of these. It immediately became clear to us that our budget targets should get a new home. We would simply move financial targets from the budget over to the financial perspective in the scorecard.

From Absolute to Relative Performance

It was not enough just to move financial targets over to the scorecard. We also had to do something with the way we set these targets. You will remember that one of our three objectives was to decentralize decisions and authority. Our traditional way of setting budget targets had been very much the opposite. It had not been enough for us to tell the business units what kind of financial performance we wanted. We also had to tell them *how* to deliver, through detailed sales, cost, personnel, and investment budgets.

We got out of this simply by limiting our financial target setting to improving return on capital employed (ROCE). Which levers to pull to lift ROCE would, within some limits, be up to the business units themselves to decide (i.e., cost, income, working capital, fixed assets). We were well aware of how this KPI potentially could discourage growth by focusing on short-term profitability only. We balanced this by also introducing such KPIs as production and market-share growth.

But there was another problem: the cyclicality of the petro-chemicals business. Veterans in the company claimed there was a seven-year cycle between boom and bust in the industry. That might have been the case historically, but we experienced a market where prices and margins were on a much faster roller coaster ride, with no sign of any seven-year cycle. (See Exhibit 3.5.)

How could we set meaningful ROCE targets in such an environment? What is good performance when prices are extremely

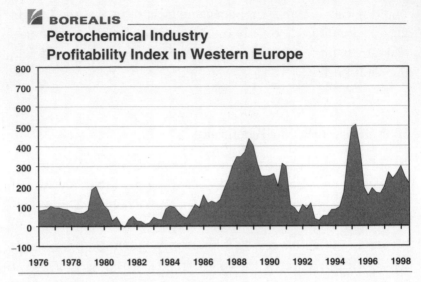

EXHIBIT 3.5 Petrochemical Profitability Index
Source: Chem Systems

volatile, but also given in a commodity market you cannot influence? Of course, you can beat market prices by a few cents.
But the overall price level was both uncontrollable and unpredictable. No wonder we got our price assumptions terribly
wrong in both the 1994 and 1995 budgets.

The solution we developed was the *relative ROCE*. This was
not a ROCE benchmarking between units, because we felt the
business units were too different. We calculated the historical
relationship between market conditions and ROCE performance
both for the company and for each of the business units. For
most units, the relationship between the two was quite linear.
Low market margins resulted in low ROCE and vice versa. Performance had nothing to do with riding up and down this line
depending on market conditions. Performance was about lifting
the relative ROCE independently of a strong or weak market.
This became the new way of setting targets. All the levers that

could improve ROCE were available for the business units to pull:

- Invest in profitable projects.
- Divest nonprofitable assets.
- Optimize working capital.
- Optimize fixed cost.
- Optimize variable cost.
- Increase margin versus market.
- Increase volumes.

Exhibit 3.6 illustrates the concept.

Relative ROCE was a tangible and effective way of saying good-bye to micromanagement. The business units were suspicious in the beginning. Do we really have this freedom and authority? And no budget constraints? Our answer was a clear yes, within certain boundaries. These included first of all the

We must improve and measure our financial performance independently of market cyclicality

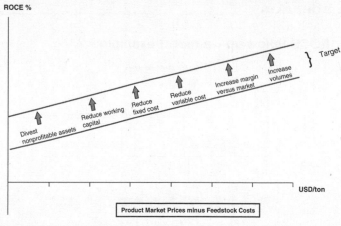

EXHIBIT 3.6 Relative Financial Performance

Borealis values, where no compromises were accepted. We also had a set of common decision criteria and clear decision authorities expressed in a mandate structure. These were wide enough to allow units to make most decisions themselves, although all larger and strategic investments were still to be brought to top management for approval.

All external financing was, of course, centralized. So were our information technology and other support processes. It was *business* freedom we wanted to provide, not the freedom for anyone to go out and buy their own accounting system. This distinction is important. It is possible to be centralized and de-centralized at the same time: centralized on common processes and support operations, and decentralized on business decisions. A common accounting system actually supports one of the Beyond Budgeting principles: *transparency* through common and open systems where performance information is visible and accessible for everyone across the company.

Exhibit 3.7 is an example on how we reported against relative ROCE targets. This illustration reflects a unit that so far has achieved an improvement of 0.6% against a 2% target. The

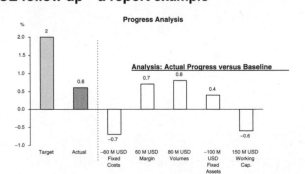

EXHIBIT 3.7 Business Follow Up

analysis explains which levers the unit has pulled. Note the "negative" development in fixed costs. Some of this might actually have been "good costs"—for instance, sales costs that lifted both volumes and margins even more than the increased sales costs. We wanted to provide to the business the freedom to decide on these kinds of trade-offs.

Benchmarking was another way of driving performance. We had about 30 production plants across Europe that benchmarked their own performance with similar plants inside and outside the company. It is amazing to observe the power of such comparisons. For those coming out low, there is always the initial denial phase: "This can't be true. We are different, the data are inaccurate," and so on. But when a unit comes out low not only in one but in several league standings, and not once but over and over again, the message ultimately tends to sink in and trigger some remarkable effects. I recall some of our plant managers, famous for their cost budget negotiation skills (perhaps why they were low in cost league standings). When they finally accepted that there was some truth in these standings, something clicked. Suddenly they wanted to move from bottom to top almost overnight. Our job became to hold them back and place them on a somewhat more realistic improvement schedule. That was a new experience, both for them and us!

Trend Reporting

Like much in the Borealis model, trend reporting was nothing new. We wanted to use trend reporting as a way of breaking out of the calendar-year prison. We accepted that statutory reporting still had to follow the calendar year, but that should no longer be a straitjacket for everything else. Nothing but tradition stood in the way for taking this step. We introduced trend reporting on costs, on production, on smaller investments, and other places where it made sense. We typically looked at historical trends covering from 6 to 15 months, depending on the area.

Then we added on a small feature that turned out to be much more effective than expected. To help the reader better understand trend lines, we added the actual "% change" number in the graphs. We experimented with different periods. I believe we ended up mainly using the last 12 over the previous 12 months. This information was especially useful on costs. In the petrochemicals business, average margins are steadily declining, and production unit cost has to follow. A cost trend constantly growing at 1% might be a serious problem, even if the line in the graph looks quite flat.

Budgeting and budget reports, in comparison, tended to blur such realities, first by allowing for higher costs and later by "hiding" the increases. Even if everyone knew that costs had to come down, the budget negotiation always included a number of convincing arguments for the opposite. The result was too often higher budgets instead of lower ones. You know the game. But as soon as we started reporting, things were OK again. No worries, we are within budget!

Trend lines and "% change" numbers might not sound very advanced. Yet this constant reminder of being on a rising trend when we should have seen the opposite did something that we had never seen with traditional budget reporting: It focused attention and urgency on costs. One year it even triggered the top 40 management team to forgo half a month's salary as a symbolic contribution to help break a cost trend moving in the wrong direction. (See Exhibits 3.8 and 3.9.)

Activity Accounting

Managing costs without budgets was by far our biggest concern. We were torn between a strong belief that everything would

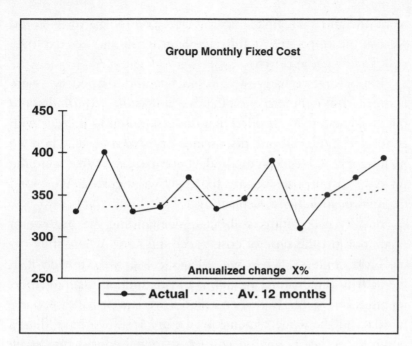

EXHIBIT 3.8 Trend Reporting Example 1

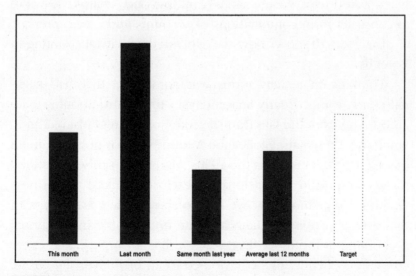

EXHIBIT 3.9 Trend Reporting Example 2

work fine and a nagging concern that refused to go away: Could we risk the opposite? As I discuss later, costs did not explode; in fact, they came down.

But before we had tested in practice and learned, we were concerned. We therefore felt that we at least had to *understand* our costs better. We needed that understanding to help us with better and more relevant discussions on *actual* costs, when we no longer could lean on the budget comparison. What were the drivers and purposes behind the costs we incurred? We found the answer in *activity accounting*.

Activity accounting is about understanding the *purpose* of costs, not just the type of costs (accounts) and where they occur (cost centers). When we discuss costs, we often do it in the activity dimension: We talk about marketing, maintenance, training, and so on. But when asked if we can provide accounting data in the same dimension, we are lost. We have details down to the last penny on *cost types* (travel, consultants, steel, power, etc.) and on cost centers: *Who* has spent the money? But when asked *why*, we are quite blank beyond what we are able to construct from combinations of accounts and cost centers.

Exhibit 3.10 shows how we explained activity accounting in Borealis.

Thinking in activity terms was something that had fascinated me from my early Statoil days. I first heard about activity accounting from the late Danish professor Vagn Madsen. Thank you to my then Statoil colleague Audun Berg for pointing me in this direction. As early as the 1950s, Madsen described the need for accounting in dimensions more closely linked to business realities. He claimed that we had to show how costs vary with the level of activity, something quite unthinkable in traditional accounting at the time. "Every action has a purpose and every cost can consequently be attributed to an objective," he wrote. He called the concept "variability accounting." I once got a lift with Madsen after a conference. He was a fascinating person,

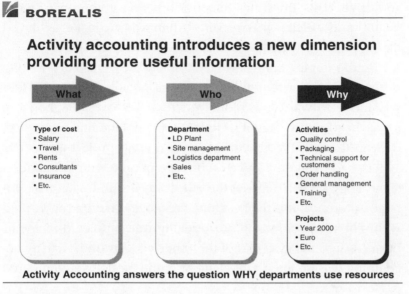

BOREALIS

Activity accounting introduces a new dimension providing more useful information

What	Who	Why
Type of cost • Salary • Travel • Rents • Consultants • Insurance • Etc.	**Department** • LD Plant • Site management • Logistics department • Sales • Etc.	**Activities** • Quality control • Packaging • Technical support for customers • Order handling • General management • Training • Etc. **Projects** • Year 2000 • Euro • Etc.

Activity Accounting answers the question WHY departments use resources

EXHIBIT 3.10 Activity Accounting

with driving skills way behind his accounting insights. He spent most of the trip through half of Denmark turned toward the two of us in the backseat, enthusiastically explaining his thinking while puffing away on his pipe.

Robert Kaplan revitalized the activity thinking and took it a long step forward with activity-based costing: ABC. By identifying the *drivers* behind the activity costs, these costs can be allocated to the *products* and *customers* driving these costs, giving a better picture of true profitability. The concept is great. The problem is that we normally have very limited activity cost data in our accounting systems. This is why activity-based product costing often is interview based. Accounting by interviewing is an approach we never would dream of practicing in our statutory accounting. Imagine walking around at year-end, asking people how much they believe they have sold and how much they have spent. I am not sure the auditors would be thrilled. Of course we do not need accounting quality on all activity and driver data. But if this dimension is important for us, more quality and efficiency is required than what can be achieved through interviewing and similar manual data collection.

Before implementing SAP, Statoil had a Swedish accounting system called *Horisonten* (Horizon)—a great name; the farther you move forward, the more you discover over the horizon. I was heading up Statoil's Horisonten implementation project back in the late 1980s, working with a great project team. The system had been developed by finance people with information technology knowledge, not the other way around. That makes a huge difference. It is the best finance system I have ever worked with. The philosophy and functionality was simple: Model your business into the system, not the other way around. Activity accounting was an important element in the model we configured in Horisonten.

Vagn Madsen was way ahead of his time. In the 1950s and 1960s, no accounting systems were able to handle the multidimensional concept he was describing. That all changed with a new generation of Swedish accounting systems emerging in the 1970s and 1980s, such as EPOK, EPOS, and later Horisonten. These systems allowed companies and business units to reflect their own business reality and management model. In Horisonten, you could add on as many independent dimensions as needed beyond accounts and cost centers, such as activity, project, profit center, and customer. On each of these dimensions, as many flags, or sorting criteria, as needed could be defined. This functionality covered any need for building multiple and parallel hierarchies or any other additional sorting of information. If you believe SAP can do the same, forget it.

The Borealis business was different from Statoil's, including a much stronger need for integration on transaction level, from production to customer. Due to this and other reasons, SAP was selected as the Borealis system. Statoil made the same choice a few years later.

In Borealis, the trigger for introducing activity accounting was also a need for *understanding* costs better. We started off by designing a common "chart of activities" to complement the chart of accounts. That turned out to be more difficult than expected, and it took us quite some time to agree on which activities to include, as well as their definitions. We finally succeeded in describing our total costs base through a list of about 100 activities. This included activities such as order handling, maintenance, quality control, training, and so on. Take training. We wanted to record all costs related to training. Earlier these costs had been recorded only by cost center and the relevant account, such as conference fees, travel, and consultants, with no possibility to trace their original purpose. Now we would also code and register the activity, in this case training.

We got a major challenge when we tried to build this third activity dimension into SAP, which basically is a two-dimensional system. We managed somehow, but not in a very elegant way. The nightmare began, however, when we also wanted the system to charge the activity information further onto products and customers. The theory was simple, as illustrated in Exhibit 3.11.

This second step became so complicated in SAP that we had to back out again a few years later. I take full responsibility for that mistake. Nevertheless, activity accounting was still useful for us. During my years in HR, I managed the function's group-wide HR cost through a report that listed our costs across 15 to 20 activities and projects. The report also showed where costs had occurred, and on which accounts, but the main focus was activity.

I still do not understand why companies put so little emphasis on this important dimension. Maybe it is another example of the external statutory accounting mind-set setting the scene for how we organize our internal finance processes, just as with the calendar year.

BOREALIS

Costs are assigned from activities to what drives them

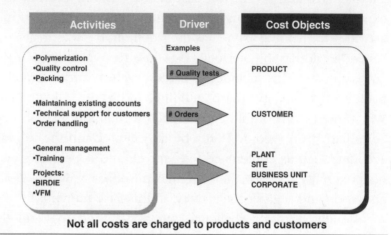

Not all costs are charged to products and customers

EXHIBIT 3.11 From Activities to Drivers

Investment Management

Capital allocation without annual budgets was almost a no-brainer. The starting point was the relative ROCE, with profitable investments as one of several levers available for the business units. In addition, we created three investments categories:

1. **Small projects** were treated more or less like operating costs, even if accounting-wise they classified as investments.
2. **Medium-size projects** were decided case by case. The hurdle rate was meant to be the lever to pull if we needed to take down the total investment level in this category. In practice, this mechanism was never used explicitly. When money was tight, there were simply fewer proposals coming forward.

3. **Major strategic projects** had never been managed through annual budgets. These projects could be acquisitions, new plants, or other major capital commitments. Such decisions seldom fit any autumn decision scheme. They were made as needed, using the best and most recent information we had on financial capacity and commercial assumptions.

When a project was approved, the investment number used in the project valuation became the cost mandate or budget for the project. So even if we still had project budgets, we cut out the annual investment budget.

The rolling financial forecast gave us a continuous and updated view of our shorter-term financial capacity, while a longer-term forecast was made annually. The investment forecast was a combination of approved projects and projects in the pipeline. When the forecast signaled capacity constraints, the actual and planned investment level was reduced by delaying or turning down more projects. It was not a very advanced and sophisticated portfolio optimization process, but it worked.

Evaluation and Rewards

It was clear for us that for the new model to work, we had to connect it all the way to evaluation and rewards. At the time, I still believed that individual bonuses were good for motivation and performance. My belief in what KPIs could do for us was also stronger than it is today.

We chose a simple approach, which at least was easy to communicate and operate. Bonuses were connected to the scorecard through the number of green KPIs. "Percentage green" became a new expression in the company. The target was typically set around 80%, with a sliding scale around the target value from threshold to ceiling values. Initially there was no weighting, but after a while we introduced "golden KPIs," which counted more than others.

As expected, the bonus link focused a lot of attention on the new scorecards. But quite soon we experienced the KPI problem. The effort put into developing strategy maps and strategic objectives was not always the best. The more "activist" oriented the teams were, the more they hurried past what they saw as an academic strategic objectives discussion and into the more concrete KPI discussion. KPIs dominated, in target setting, follow-up, evaluation, and rewards, causing many of the negative side effects I talked about earlier. The emphasis on strategic objectives improved later on, but I do not think the model ever fully recovered from our initial KPI success.

Implementation Experiences and Lessons Learned

Even if the Borealis case was not a full-blown Beyond Budgeting implementation, what we did was quite radical at the time. Aside from the Handelsbanken case (which, as I have said, we had not heard of at the time), I think few other companies had jumped into the unknown the way we did. Given how early we moved, and how few we could learn from, I am proud of what we achieved. Of course, we had a great starting point. It was a new company, with change-oriented values, open-minded chief financial and chief executive officers, and a strong finance team.

Still, there are things we should have done differently. First of all, we could have articulated our vision more clearly and broadly, especially on the leadership side. We could have aimed even higher. But this is hindsight wisdom. The BBRT research and model development now provides a framework that did not exist when we started out.

I also wish we had involved the HR function earlier. We did so later, when we linked the scorecard to incentives. Yet HR should have been with us from day one. I will elaborate on this point later in the book. My own days in HR were still ahead of me. I must also admit that at the time, I believed some of the rather negative myths about this function.

Our strong belief in KPIs meant that strategic objectives took the backseat. Our expectations of what KPIs could do for us were far too high. They were adjusted over the years, but these objectives never played the same role in the performance management process as they later did in the Statoil model.

The relative ROCE KPI was abandoned after some years. It lost out in the battle between relevance and precision, but probably also it was too complicated to operate. It was replaced with more absolute financial targets, but these were still set at a high level without a lot of detail.

Another consequence of being an early mover on scorecards was the lack of any supporting software. The process in Borealis was very much a manual one, supported by numerous spreadsheets. The fact that scorecards survived without any real system support may confirm how strongly anchored the concept actually was. I am glad, however, that we never tried to configure scorecards in SAP as we tried with activity costs on products and customers.

A key lesson learned came as quite a surprise to us: *Don't design everything up front*. The issues and challenges might pop up in the most unexpected areas. Design to 80% and jump, and sort out the issues as they occur. In hindsight, this should have been obvious to us, as it actually is what Beyond Budgeting is very much about. Everything cannot be planned. You have to sense and respond as you go.

At the time, our strategy was to design as much as possible before we jumped. We felt we had to, because there were so many questions coming from the organization: "How will we now do this and that without a budget?" We felt we had to answer all these questions properly in order to get people on board. Most of the questions obviously were related to cost management. Because we were quite concerned with this issue ourselves, we spent a lot of time developing activity accounting, trend reporting, mandates, and other mechanisms.

What happened? In Borealis's short budget history, costs came in above budget both in 1994 and 1995. Then we abolished budgets, but costs did not explode. In fact, they came down. I do not think this happened because of our thorough work up front. Also, I am not crediting the cost reduction only to the fact that we took away cost budgets. Obviously integration costs were disappearing and synergies were kicking in. But I do believe that what we experienced had a lot to do with people being much more responsible than what traditional management preaches.

So the first challenge did not occur on cost management, as we had expected. We actually got it in a very different area, in *investment forecasting*. For us, the rolling financial forecasts had been a no-brainer. We had explained again and again to the organization that a forecast should reflect the expected outcome and nothing else. It should *not* be an application for funds, because this would be handled in a separate process. Everyone nodded and agreed that it absolutely made sense to distinguish between these two very different purposes.

Then came the big day when we had consolidated our first rolling financial forecast. It was an important milestone, and our excitement about what the numbers looked like was sky high. It all seemed OK, until we came to the investment forecast. That number was maybe two or three times higher than any previous investment level ever seen in the company, and way above our financial and organizational capacity.

It was not difficult to understand what had happened. Our message had been understood but not fully believed. It had not translated into any change in behavior. What we had in front of us was not a forecast but a solid application for investment money. We had asked line controllers to be careful with challenging the numbers on their way up, to avoid giving an impression of just another budget process. So we were sitting on a massive and unfiltered pile of investment proposals.

We had two choices regarding the numbers to take to the executive committee later that week: We could go back to the organization and negotiate the numbers down to a more reasonable level. We knew, however, too well what the response would be: "You are coming to cut our investments? So much for a new process!"

We therefore chose the opposite tack. We took the inflated numbers with us to the executive committee without any adjustments. The response came fast from the CEO: "This is nonsense!" "We know," we replied, "but this is the forecast we got from the business areas sitting around this table." The room became dead silent. Later we adjusted the numbers, without telling the organization. The next quarter almost the same thing happened, but this time with somewhat lower numbers. It took four rounds and four quarters before the organization finally had internalized that these numbers were about forecasting only, not about investment proposals and funding.

Abolishing budgets turned out to be an even more positive experience for the finance function than we had expected. In addition to all the benefits for the company, we also enjoyed less number crunching and much more interesting work. But we also experienced a remarkable effect on our *image* in the organization. To begin with, our image was similar to the image of most finance teams. There was not too much respect for our business understanding or our ability to add value. When we first proposed to kick out the budgets, many Borealis managers were confused and quite suspicious about our motives. Why would these guys want to give up their number-one power instrument? they wondered. What was our hidden agenda? When they finally realized that there were no hidden agendas, that our only goal was to benefit the company, our standing and image got a major boost. It took us a big step forward toward that business partner role that most finance functions, and now also HR, strive so hard to achieve.

The Borealis implementation was an important part of my own history when Statoil embarked on a similar journey 10 years later. Experiences from both these cases are summarized in Chapter 5, where I present a seven-point implementation strategy that should be relevant whatever business you are in.

Borealis Today

The Borealis years were a fantastic experience, and something I am extremely grateful for having been part of. It was a great time with great people in a great company. Borealis was a real pioneer, driving change in a number of areas, not just within performance management.

And the changes continued. In 1998 Neste sold out as part of a strategic reorientation. Austrian OMV and IPIC of Abu Dhabi came in. OMV had its own European petrochemicals business, PCD, so now it was integration time again. Svein Rennemo took over as the new CEO. I was asked to head up the integration project and took a leave from my finance role. Although on a much smaller scale, the project had some similarities with the Statoil-Hydro merger 10 years later. The Borealis name was kept, but the intention was a true merger between equals, even if PCD was a much smaller company. The integration work included a completely new organizational structure with new management teams at all levels, especially in sales, marketing, logistics, research and development, and other areas with significant overlaps and synergies. We got a lot of positive feedback on how the integration was executed from both old and new Borealis colleagues, even from many of those who had to leave the company. For me, this was another major learning experience, which continued when I was asked to head up HR after we had gone live with the new company.

There was, however, tension brewing between old and new owners. This went well beyond the constructive discussions and occasional disagreements between Statoil and Neste. Svein Rennemo left Borealis in 2001. I left half a year later, after a conflict with his successor. I have a lot of respect for the new CEO's drive and the ambitious goals he set for the company, but we had different views on how to get there.

Statoil divested its Borealis shareholding in 2005. The company has now moved its head office from Copenhagen to Vienna and has also sold its Norwegian assets. Today Borealis is firmly under the wings of its main shareholder, Austrian OMV, which again is partly controlled from Abu Dhabi. The Nordic roots are not that visible anymore. The company is expanding in the Middle East, through a strong position in the Abu Dhabi joint venture Borouge.

Borealis today seems to have taken a few steps back on its Beyond Budgeting journey, although not all the way back. Most of the new processes still exist, such as the balanced scorecard and the rolling forecasts. My impression is, however, that there is now more of a traditional management culture compared to how the company was run in the 1990s. Why this happened is probably a book in itself. Personally, I believe it had something to do with a number of new external recruits to the executive committee, starting with the new CEO. These were all bright guys, but they had not been part of the original journey. Without that history, perhaps they found it difficult to understand and fully appreciate the leadership principles and the underlying intentions of the model.

It is obvious that the greater the changes in top management a company goes through, the longer a Beyond Budgeting model must be in operation to survive. This is especially true if few in the new team are from the company's own ranks. It takes years for these kinds of process changes to find their way into the hearts and minds of people and to be reflected in behavior and leadership. The transformation was well under way in Borealis, but an eight-year journey may not have been long enough to balance the effect of so many new guys at the top.

How long does it take for Beyond Budgeting to take root, to become so strong that it survives the kind of changes that Borealis went through? I do not think anyone knows yet. We know that Handelsbanken has been going since 1970 and seems to have a rock-solid foundation. But there are very few other old cases that can tell us how long it takes before the walls are thick enough to resist a few earthquakes.

Some may argue that the Borealis model primarily addressed the *process* side and less the *leadership* side of Beyond Budgeting and that this made it less robust against later management changes. I partly agree. It is true that our starting point was the budget itself and the problems that most directly originated from this area. But we clearly saw and addressed leadership implications such as autonomy, transparency, and values. For instance, the value focus was extremely strong from day one.

We can speculate whether differences between a Nordic and a German/Austrian culture played a role. The Nordic culture is still present in Borealis, with significant Swedish and Finnish operations, but these countries have no ownership role. It should, however, be noted that an increasing number of large German companies have started on a Beyond Budgeting journey, companies including UBS, Aldi, Hilti, dm-drogerie markt, and Egon Zendher. A fresh and fascinating case is the small German company Paradigma, operating in the green energy business. I look forward to following this case further.

Borealis had a great start in 1994. The company had the potential and was on its way toward a comprehensive and robust Beyond Budgeting model, but the changes at the top were simply too great and came too quickly. If something similar had happened in Handelsbanken in 1978, after a similar eight-year journey, perhaps that bank would look quite different today. Handelsbanken has a policy of recruiting top management from within, which makes a big difference. We should all be thankful that their journey continues, because we need more of those experienced seniors with so many young guys on the scene.

I still have many friends in Borealis. I wish each of them all the best wherever their journey heads. Together, we made a difference!

CHAPTER 4

The Statoil Case

Introduction

Sharing the Statoil case is quite different from sharing the Borealis case. The last one is behind me, and long enough behind to allow for the necessary reflection and learning. The Statoil case is still a work in progress. Although we have been on our Beyond Budgeting journey for several years now, we still are as I write and probably also as you read.

Statoil was established in 1972 as a national oil company following the discovery of significant oil and gas reserves on the Norwegian continental shelf in the late 1960s. The company grew fast during the 1970s and 1980s, taking a number of brave steps in both technology and project development. The international activities were turbocharged through an alliance with BP in the 1990s, which accessed a number of key strategic assets in several countries including Angola, Nigeria, and Azerbaijan. In 2001 Statoil went public with a listing in New York and Oslo, although the state kept a majority shareholding. Statoil quickly became an attractive investment due to a track record of combined growth and profitability.

In 2007 Statoil merged with the oil and gas division of Hydro, a Norwegian competitor. StatoilHydro is Scandinavia's largest company, with 31,000 employees across 41 countries and a turnover and market cap well above $100 billion. The company is the world's largest offshore operator, the second largest gas supplier to Europe, and the world's third largest crude oil seller. The rationale behind the merger was to combine forces to further strengthen international growth. The strategy has already paid off, for instance, through the award of a 24% ownership share in Shtokman, the world's largest offshore gas field, located in Arctic Russia, a project the two companies had competed separately for.

According to the merger agreement, Statoil's performance management process was to be used in the new company. But as in any marriage, partners influence each other and find their new way together. This is a natural point in time to take stock of the Statoil case and how far we got before the merger. So consider this chapter to be a status report on a journey that by no means is over. On a few occasions, you will find me talking also about StatoilHydro, as part of this book is being written during the early days of the new company.

The Statoil story does not have the same speed and defining moments as we experienced in Borealis. Statoil was a much larger company. Although still a youngster, it had a history and a legacy that the newborn Borealis, with its key value of "One company—new, different and better," did not have.

On May 9, 2005, Statoil's executive committee formally decided to abolish traditional budgeting and replace it with a new philosophy backed by new processes. Up until this point, the journey had been one of gradual and steady change. Throughout the 1990s, brick by brick had been laid onto a foundation that finally was robust enough to carry the weight of more radical change. From here on, we accelerated the building activities significantly. Our vision of what kind of house we wanted to build also became more ambitious as we moved on.

Creating the Foundation

During the 1990s Statoil took several important steps that together paved the way for the 2005 decision. Most of these took
place under the guidance and leadership of Eldar Sætre, who
held several key finance positions before becoming chief financial officer (CFO) in Statoil and later in StatoilHydro. I reported
to Eldar in my first management job in Statoil back in 1984,
heading up the budget department, where I had joined the
company a year earlier.

I was busy in Borealis when much of these changes
were taking place. The steps taken ranged from culture and
competence to process and systems. A strong and professional finance network was built. The network was glued together with common and group-wide finance systems and
processes, regular network meetings and conferences, functional competence development, and a strong corporate involvement in key finance role appointments in the line. An
important step was to redefine the controller role toward an
active business partner, adviser, and challenger to business
teams. To support this new role, most transactional tasks were
moved over to Global Business Services, Statoil's shared service center. By this move, the line controller no longer had
to deal with data production and much of the basic data
analysis.

In 1997 Statoil went for a large-scale SAP implementation.
The project included work process standardization around three
core principles:

1. Same business—same process
2. Cost responsibility moved from resource owner to task responsible
3. From budget management to scorecard management

Already at this time there were thoughts and intentions about doing something with the budget process. For different reasons, the effort ended with some simplifications only and little real change. The budget problem was not yet fully understood. Few other companies had declared war on the budget. Also, the balanced scorecard initiative did not really take off as intended. It was a manual process, focused on group and business area levels. It was a start, but initially not a major success. The budget survived very much intact. "We were simply not ready yet," as Eldar Sætre puts it today.

Moving from cost center to task responsibility was a version of the activity accounting introduced in the Horisonten system 10 years earlier. The purpose was to ensure a continued activity focus and robustness against constant organizational changes. Below the business unit level, cost responsibilities were assigned around tasks and processes that reflected the company's value chain. Cost centers became *resource owners*, holding the employer role. People's time and cost were posted on tasks for which different business units were responsible. Although cost centers went through continuous organizational change, the tasks and processes the organization worked on remained relatively stable. The highest level in this task structure looked like Exhibit 4.1.

At the time, this was one of the largest SAP projects in Europe. Compared to many other similar projects, it was a success. It also created something that became crucial for later developments: a common set of business data in the data warehouse module of SAP.

In 2000 another scorecard exercise started, this time in a different place. In one of the business areas, Exploration and Production Norway, there was a strong wish for better information and support around daily operations. My good friend and colleague Arvid Hollevik was in charge of this project, which originated in the unit responsible for the gigantic Troll field.

A value-chain based task structure

Aquire resources	Project development	Operations and supply	Sales and distribution	Competence and services
• Business development • Product development • Market development • Portfolio optimization • Area acquisition • Resource proving • Commercialization	• Development • Operations preparation • Drilling and completion • Modifications • Removal	• Operations and maintenance • Reservoir management • Well maintenance • Health, environment, and safety • Logistics, warehouse, and material administration • Laboratory work • Production management • Production fees	• Sales • Marketing • Transportation • Distribution • Category management • Customer management	• Administrative support • Head office and research and development charges • Fees • Products • Common services

Additional "expenditure type" category available for all tasks:

• **Continuous**
• **Year specific**
• **Categories of investment**

StatoilHydro

EXHIBIT 4.1 Task Structure

The challenge was not a lack of measurement. The place was full of key performance indicators (KPIs)—in fact, far too many. Many were almost identical, but always with slightly different definitions. Collecting and distributing KPI data was a manual and time-consuming process.

This business-driven project became the start of the management information system MIS: "Management Information in StatoilHydro," as the full name reads today. It is an in-house application, a web interface built on top of the SAP data warehouse. The main purpose at that time was to provide front-line teams with better information, primarily on operational indicators, and help them manage their own business with faster and more relevant data and with less dependence on outside staff.

Most scorecard implementations start at the top and are cascaded out into the organization. They are also mainly about translating and communicating group strategies. The earlier corporate scorecard initiative was in this top-down category and was now struggling. It was run by the central finance function in a manual process, and its main focus still was on group and business areas only. The idea of less central control was not very prominent. Reports to the executive committee and the board included KPIs but could hardly be called a full scorecard. The original good intentions of this project were slowly fading.

MIS was more of a *bottom-up* phenomenon. Rumors spread, and after some time the whole "Exploration and Production Norway" business area decided to implement MIS. It did not take long before other business areas became interested. International Exploration came onboard, as did Manufacturing and Marketing, Natural Gas, Global Business Services, and finally Corporate Staffs. Following this rapid growth, the obvious decision was made in 2004 that MIS would become a group system. This was not seen as a top-down implementation but as a natural consequence of the successful growth from the front line up.

At the same time, the scope of MIS was growing. The vision became to make this the "management portal" in Statoil. New reports and information were continuously added: benchmarking data, activity follow-up, partner reporting, internal supplier/customer relations and transactions.

As a consequence of being listed in the United States, the company has to follow the Sarbanes-Oxley (SOX) regulations. MIS provides a continuously updated status on all SOX key controls in the company. Without an automated follow-up, SOX requirements can choke any company. An increasing number of companies are leaving U.S. stock exchanges because of SOX. BP's CEO, Tony Hayward, put it like this: "Assurance is killing us."

I must admit I am quite skeptical regarding much of what SOX represents and many of the controls we have put in place in order to be SOX compliant. Fortunately, the pendulum seems to be swinging back already. Controls are now being cut or simplified compared to what we started out with. The whole Sarbanes-Oxley Act is actually a good example of management versus leadership. It was triggered by serious violations of ethics and value standards. The American response was more police on the streets, more new rules and regulations, instead of addressing the underlying problem: ethics and values. I am often asked about how we can promote Beyond Budgeting while at the same time introducing SOX in the company. My answer is that there will always be forces pulling in different directions in any organization. With SOX around, we need Beyond Budgeting more than ever!

But back to the MIS history. Along the way, Ambition to action was born. It started out as a place in MIS to document strategic objectives, KPIs, and actions for local units. It was a voluntary exercise, aimed at helping teams develop their KPIs and document their work. At the time it was not actively used in any subsequent follow-up and was not brought to full life until several years later. You will hear a lot more about Ambition to action shortly.

Arvid Hollevik has been the driver behind the MIS system from day one. He has been everywhere in the organization, preaching, teaching, pulling, and teasing people onboard the thinking and the system. He has also driven the broadening of the system functionality, always one step ahead, seeing new opportunities and areas where the system could be used. We could never have taken Beyond Budgeting to where we are today without the MIS platform and the work done by Arvid and his team. The two of us work closely together. People say we are quite different, which is probably why we complement each other so well. No one has challenged me harder on making a simple picture that explains what Beyond Budgeting is all about, on one page only!

After several years of continuously building and strengthening the performance management platform, the situation in 2004 was a strong one:

- A strong and united finance network
- Common data definitions across the group, from chart of accounts to KPIs
- A common SAP system and process platform
- A scorecard process built from below over several years, supported by a great MIS system
- An emerging finance/human resources (HR) alliance
- And last but not least, an organization with an open culture and strong values, including my personal favorite: "Challenge accepted truths and enter unfamiliar territory"

The last point is important. Statoil has always been a value-driven organization, although these values were not put on paper before the end of the 1980s. There have been a few updates since that time, but all versions have emphasized openness, honesty, and trust, combined with a strong encouragement for change and improvement. These values created an environment where challenging the status quo is both accepted and expected, especially when the challenge is supported by a proposal for a better way.

Statoil has a history of giving people wide responsibilities and challenging tasks at young age. That was simply a necessity, because the company had to hit the ground running in the early 1970s. Within 10 years, the young and rapidly growing organization had taken on challenges many other oil companies have spent much longer mastering. This trust and freedom have been instrumental in shaping the Statoil culture. I believe it also makes the company better prepared for a Beyond Budgeting journey than many of its peers.

Eldar Sætre had initiated and supported much of the finance function's development through his different key finance roles since joining Statoil in 1981. In 2004 Statoil's new CEO, Helge Lund, came onboard; he was 42 years old at the time. He picked Eldar as CFO, a role he had been acting in for a year already. A new head of HR, Jens R. Jenssen, was also recruited.

The platform was in place. Statoil was ready to take its performance management process to the next level.

Starting Out

I returned from Borealis in 2002 and started as corporate controller working toward the International Exploration & Production business area (INT), with Eldar Sætre as my manager once again. It was a great job and a great time. Statoil's growth had to take place internationally. The Norwegian continental shelf is a relatively mature oil and gas region. Holding the fort and maintaining current production levels is job number one. INT is therefore charged with realizing the growth ambition. The business area had already secured substantial international production through the now-terminated BP alliance but was still very much a project-driven organization, chasing growth opportunities around the world. My main responsibility was to challenge and advise on new projects and business opportunities. I was also coordinating the budgeting and planning process between the corporate center and INT. Compared to the sister unit responsible for the Norwegian continental shelf, INT operates in an even more dynamic and unpredictable environment. This provided us with a wealth of great examples and evidence why traditional budgeting and planning is a flawed process.

INT was not afraid of aiming high and taking on challenging targets. Securing access to capital and internal resources was a high priority. It definitely influenced the proposed budget and planning numbers, and in one direction only. I recall one year, when the first input on long-term production profiles and required investments were sky high. We all knew these numbers were not even close to reflecting any expected outcome. As a challenging ambition they made much more sense, by stretching and firing up the organization. But the process only allowed for one number to represent both an ambitious target and a realistic expected outcome. It was simply impossible. Not surprisingly, the result was a negotiated compromise, an "in-between number" that nobody was very happy about.

Another favorite discussion was country office costs. At the time, most country offices were cost centers, a "hotel" and a service provider for the various businesses with activity in the country. All business units wanted country offices to be managed tightly through detailed cost budgets, because they were picking up the bill through cost allocations. A lot of time and energy was spent each year negotiating the "right" cost budget and detailed allocation keys, with active senior involvement from each of the "hotel guests."

Then the year started and reality hit. Suddenly a business opportunity emerged. It could be an acquisition opportunity, a farm-in offer, or something similar. They often came out of the blue, and seldom could they be planned for. I was always impressed with how quickly and professionally the business units grabbed these opportunities, which often involved significant costs and activity peaks also for the actual country office. When these opportunities occurred, the business units had forgotten all about last year's budget negotiations. Now the focus was where it should be: on making the right and necessary efforts to secure the deal, even if doing so had cost implications beyond agreed budgets. But when autumn came, it was back to the negotiation table, quarreling about next year's budget and allocation keys.

Another favorite of mine was the exploration budget. Before I share this, I want to underline that I am not criticizing the Global Exploration management team. They are great people, and I highly respect the job they do. I am criticizing the system we asked them to operate under. They did not invent it, we did.

The list of arguments for why next year's exploration budget had to be bigger than last year's was always long and convincing. But more as a rule than an exception, the unit came back at year-end, announcing that it was "giving money back to the company." The budget the team had fought so hard for had not been spent. As you will recall, we also had balanced scorecards at the time. These were very much KPI dominated. An important KPI on the Global Exploration scorecard was "exploration costs versus budget." Even I, who struggle with colors and especially with separating red and green, was able to see that this KPI was shining green. The scorecard was also connected to the bonus system. The greener the KPIs, the higher the bonus.

It was not difficult to understand why the exploration budget had not been spent. The main reasons were about not entering new exploration areas as planned (which cost a lot of money) and about delays in exploration drilling. None of this could really be called good performance, even if some of the reasons might have been outside the control of Global Exploration. Still, we managed to turn all of this into good performance, through the very misleading KPI "exploration costs versus budget." Those days are gone. I will explain what we now do a bit later.

There is another fascinating side of this story. By giving Global Exploration a bag of money each year, we stated with high self-confidence that *this* was the right dose of resources to put into international exploration next year. That part we were pretty certain about. The amount was seldom a round number. It should reflect the fact that there were loads of details and tough negotiations behind. At the same time, we made no secret of all the uncertainty ahead: which additional new exploration opportunities might pop up, the complicated rig scheduling, or what the drilling rig rates would be, just to name a few. (Those rig rates have, by the way, tripled and more in just a few years.) All this uncertainty and more we openly acknowledged, but still we knew exactly the right amount of money to spend!

My colleagues brought similar stories from other business areas. The list of examples illustrating the problem with current practices became longer and longer. We spent more and more time discussing what we observed and increasingly also *why* all this happened. In these discussions, I often referred to what we had done in Borealis. I should have stopped doing that much earlier. It must have been both irritating and tiring for my colleagues to listen to me banging on about the Borealis case, a company they had little relation to. Looking back, I realize how patient they were. I forgot an important principle: Everybody needs his own journey. If roles had been switched, I probably would have asked the guy to shut up.

Our discussions continued throughout 2003 and 2004. Gradually a shared understanding emerged about the underlying problems and also sketches of possible alternatives. The appetite for addressing the problems in a radical way was increasing. The team became more and more confident that there was an alternative, a different model that actually would work. In early 2005 we were ready to take a proposal to the executive committee. On May 9 we got the green light, with strong backing from the CEO and CFO. Eldar Sætre was, of course, familiar with the history and the platform building. In one way it was a bigger leap of faith for the new CEO, Helge Lund. He demonstrated a lot of trust, both toward his CFO and toward us and the rest of the organization.

Shortly afterward, I moved into a full-time Beyond Budgeting project manager role. Steve Morlidge, who held a similar role in Unilever, claims that there were only three of us in such roles at the time. The third one, according to him, was in the World Bank in New York. I am glad that number is on the way up. Right now there are actually three of us in Norway alone. Both the world's seventh largest telecom company, Telenor, and the bank Sparebank1 Gruppen are on now the journey, with full-time project managers.

The Statoil Model

Introduction

Before we move into the Statoil model, I want to remind you that what follows is a description of the model as we designed it. The main challenge never lies in design but in implementation. How far we have come depends on which glasses you put on and where you are in the organization. We have a clear decision behind us, and we have strong support from the CEO and CFO. The board has not approved a budget since 2004. The corporate center applies the full model toward all of the business areas. A lot of units are fully onboard and have been operating the entire model for several years now. But we also have units and managers who still seem to have a foot in the old world, and there are also those with the entire mind and body still firmly rooted in the past. That does not necessarily mean that they are not using the new tools and processes. It is the *way* these are used that sometimes resembles traditional management more than Beyond Budgeting principles. We have also just been through a merger, which for some parts of the organization means starting over again with training and implementation.

But compared to most other companies, or compared to where we started out in 2005, we have moved mountains, and we will keep doing so because we are eating a piece of the elephant every day. I do not want to tell you a sanitized story where everything is solved and everything is perfect. Those cases might exist in books and in fancy conference presentations, but seldom in the real world. There is more about this in the closing remarks in Chapter 5.

When people outside the company hear that we have abolished budgeting, the immediate question is always "What do you do instead?" I do not like to answer that question before I have had a chance to explain what we wanted to get away from and, more important, what we want to move toward. Our model can be fully understood only if that background and those objectives also are understood.

In the thousands of internal presentations on the new model we have held during the last years, we always try to start with two pictures. The first is a short summary of the main problems with budgeting, shown in Exhibit 4.2. There are many ways of

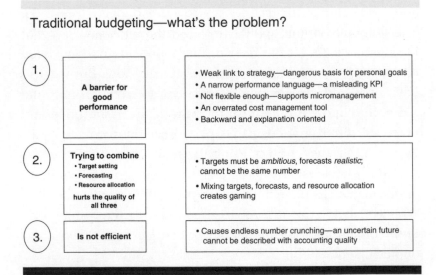

Traditional budgeting—what's the problem?

1. **A barrier for good performance**
   - Weak link to strategy—dangerous basis for personal goals
   - A narrow performance language—a misleading KPI
   - Not flexible enough—supports micromanagement
   - An overrated cost management tool
   - Backward and explanation oriented

2. **Trying to combine**
   - Target setting
   - Forecasting
   - Resource allocation
   hurts the quality of all three
   - Targets must be *ambitious*, forecasts *realistic*; cannot be the same number
   - Mixing targets, forecasts, and resource allocation creates gaming

3. **Is not efficient**
   - Causes endless number crunching—an uncertain future cannot be described with accounting quality

StatoilHydro

EXHIBIT 4.2 The Budget Problems

Key principles

- Performance is ultimately about **outperforming peers**.
- **Do the right thing** in the actual situation, guided by the StatoilHydro Book, your Ambition to action, decision criteria and authorities, and sound business judgment.
- Within this framework, **resources** are available or allocated case by case.
- Business follow-up is **forward looking** and **action** oriented.
- Performance evaluation is a **holistic** assessment of delivery *and* behavior.

StatoilHydro

EXHIBIT 4.3 Key Principles

illustrating these problems. As a one-pager, this one has worked quite well. You will recognize the problems from our previous discussions. Note that we have placed the efficiency problem last, to underline that this is not the main problem.

The next picture, shown in Exhibit 4.3, summarizes some of the key principles in the new model. I do not think Arvid is 100% satisfied yet, but it works quite well. Many people are surprised when they see this for the first time, because they find it not very finance oriented, which is exactly the point.

You will recognize the thinking behind many of these statements. Some people struggle with the "Do the right thing..." statement. After we have defined good performance, this one tries to address an even more important question: How do we *get* good performance? Thousands of books try to answer that question. We do not claim to have the ultimate answer. But we believe that if people do the right things in all the situations they face every day, then that is a pretty good starting point for getting good performance. This includes the many situations we can never foresee in our budgets and business plans. If the right decisions are taken and also executed well, it is not unlikely that we as a company also will perform quite well. We believe those decisions often are best taken by those closest to the situation. To do this, however, people in the front line must have sufficient authority and responsibility. People need *room to move*.

We have made that room much bigger, but we are not talking anarchy without boundaries. The room still has walls. The first wall in the larger "room to move" is the StatoilHydro book, a booklet that is given to everyone in the company, that basically says how we do things in StatoilHydro. (See Exhibit 4.4.) It starts out where it should start, with values and leadership principles. Then it becomes a bit more concrete, describing our Operating Model including the Ambition to action process. The book also includes some key corporate policies, but it is not a huge instruction book. It provides guidance and direction, not microinstructions.

The *second wall* is each unit's Ambition to action. This provides more concrete guidance and direction through strategic objectives, KPIs, and actions. You will read a lot more about Ambition to action in a minute.

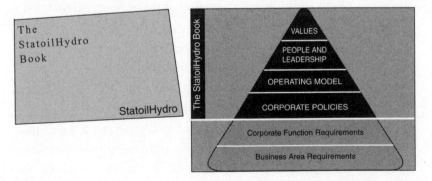

EXHIBIT 4.4 StatoilHydro Book

The *third wall* is a structured decision process, with a common set of decision criteria for projects and major new activities at defined decision gates as a project matures toward a final decision. This is combined with decision authorities, stating how big an individual decision a manager can make before having to go one level up. This wall has been there all the time. What is new is that we no longer have "double decision making" by also approving annual budgets.

The *fourth wall* is sound business judgment. The power of common sense should never be underestimated. I mistrust any model that lacks this key component.

Within this framework, resources are, in principle, available for running operations, regulated by mechanisms you will read more about in the "Dynamic Resource Allocation" section later on. For larger projects and major new activities, we still set cost targets based on the financial evaluation of the project. We do this, however, only when the funding is needed, and not also in an additional autumn preallocation. The bank is open 12 months a year, not just 4 weeks in October. But your "loan application" still can be turned down. It has *not* become easier to get a project approved; rather the opposite, because "It is already in my budget" is no longer an argument.

All the five key principles will be explained more in detail later on, including the dynamic resource allocation, the forward- and action-oriented business follow-up, and the holistic performance evaluation.

Before we move on, a word of warning. Many of you will find our model disappointingly simple, with many elements that may already be a part of your own model. What we believe we do differently lies in part in what we no longer do: traditional budgeting. The way we operate what might be seen as standard components in a performance management process also makes a difference. Having a balanced scorecard is not unique at all. The way it is implemented and operated, however, makes a big difference. A scorecard can protect and reinforce a command-and-control regime, or it can do the opposite. Too many companies are in the first category. We aim to be in the second.

The way it all hangs together and how we have *integrated* the different steps in the performance management process also make a difference. The parts are not unique, but they are well connected, from strategy to people, from center to front line. Finally, we have something we believe is better than what many other companies have—at least that is what people outside the company keep telling us—the backing of great systems like MIS and our HR system: People@StatoilHydro, which covers the "people" part of the performance management process, as described later on.

But again, you might still be disappointed. And fair enough, because there is no rocket science involved, just a lot of common sense.

Ambition to Action

Ambition to action is our version of the balanced scorecard and also the name of our integrated performance management process, which runs all the way from strategy to business management and into individual goals, evaluation, and rewards.

Although it might look like a standard scorecard, we believe there are four reasons why Ambition to action has something more to it than the typical scorecard:

1. We did not just put it on top of what we already had. We also took something away. The budget was a serious competitor, which almost always won when the two concepts collided. When budgets were removed, it was a strong signal to the organization that we now are serious about Ambition to action, because that is all there is.

2. We have worked hard to prevent Ambition to action from becoming just another command-and-control tool from the top, by trying to find the right balance between central alignment and local ownership.
3. For many years, scorecards in Statoil were KPI scorecards only. A tired cynicism was emerging around KPIs, because we promoted them more than they deserved. By lifting up strategic objectives and actions alongside the KPIs, we got a broader and more meaningful arena and language for target setting, follow-up, and performance evaluation. We became less dependent on KPIs, and Ambition to action became a process that better reflected business realities and how the organization actually works.
4. We have used Ambition to action to build bridges, not just to the strategy process but also to the "people process." The focus on *integrated* performance management has been very well received in the organization, again because it better reflects reality. This integration has brought synergies well above our expectations. Ambition to action is now a household term both in strategy and in human resources.

The starting point for Ambition to action is the established strategy, where the necessary situation analysis, ambitions, and strategic direction are addressed. This is where we make the big choices. Remember, you do not have a strategy if you never say no. The purpose of Ambition to action is less about making and more about *executing* strategy, by *translating* it into something more concrete through asking such questions as:

- Where are we going, and what does success look like? (Ambition and strategic objectives)
- How do we get there? (Actions)
- How do we measure progress? (KPIs)

We ask these questions within each of the four standard balanced scorecard perspectives: finance, market, operations, and people and organization. We have however added a fifth, health, safety, and environment (HSE), due to the extreme importance of this dimension in our industry.

We have also turned the conventional order of these perspectives. Most scorecards start with the finance perspective. We start with people and organization, followed by HSE, ending with finance. We do this to ensure that the business reviews follow the cause-and-effect relation between the perspectives. Finance now comes last, as a *consequence* of the actions and deliveries on the other perspectives. When *making* an Ambition to action, however, we start with the Finance perspective and the results we want to achieve. Then we work our way backward through a cause-and-effect relation between the different drivers that lay the foundation for good financial results.

Exhibit 4.5 provides an example of a typical Ambition to action. It is from the retail business in Latvia and is taken straight out of the MIS system. As for quality, it represents an average. There are both better and worse ones.

This unit has formulated its overall ambition as "Lean retailing beyond expectations." The discussion about the right use of words like "ambition," "mission," and "vision" still pops up from time to time. For me, this discussion is a waste of energy. I do not really care what we call it. What is important is that we state something meaningful about the overall purpose or direction, a guiding star that makes people tick and provides guidance for the rest of the Ambition to action. Such a guiding star cannot have so many levels and dimensions (mission, vision, ambition, etc.) that it becomes blurred and confuses more than it guides. Actually, the majority of employees could not care less about the academic distinction between mission and vision. They just want to be inspired and ignited.

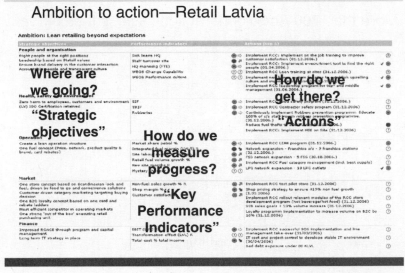

EXHIBIT 4.5 Ambition to Action

Today there are more than 700 Ambition to actions in the company, as shown in Exhibit 4.6. Most organizational units of a certain size have their own. The one on group level is what the board now approves instead of a budget. In the same meeting, the board also is shown forecasts on expected financial developments, including investment forecasts. These are for information only and are not approved. It is "fresh" information, sometimes outdated a week later. In addition, the board of course approves our largest projects, but this is done continuously and not in an annual budget.

The number of Ambition to actions keeps growing. Frontline managers constantly ask if they should use Ambition to action in their own units. Our answer is simple. There is no "corporate instruction" imposing use at these levels. We absolutely recommend trying it out, but the use should be driven

More than 700 Ambition to actions across the company

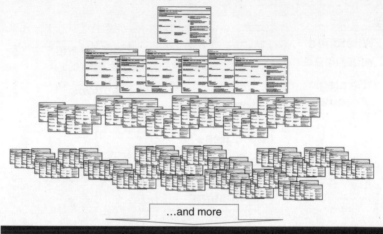

...and more

StatoilHydro

EXHIBIT 4.6 The Ambition to Action Hierarchy

because doing so makes sense for the unit itself. If people establish an Ambition to action only because they are instructed to do so from above, they might be better off without it. Too often such Ambition to actions become pure reporting channels for feeding data to levels above, with little or no active use in the unit itself. Ambition to action should be something you do more for yourself than for others. If used well in the front line, there will always be enough data and information available for those above to tap into.

The best indication of doing it for others is when Ambition to action is updated only before review meetings with the level above. We even came across a manager who believed he had to make one to be on the bonus system. I can hardly think of a worse motivation.

There is a clear expectation that the concept is applied in business areas and business units, but I do not think anyone feels forced to do so. A number of staff units have also decided to establish their own Ambition to action. In the unit where I am based, we have had one for several years. Our ambition statement is short but ambitious: "Improving business decisions—driving performance and change." This is the main reason for our existence and what we aim for. We then formulated relevant strategic objectives and concrete actions across all five perspectives. The basis and inspiration is the Ambition to action for the group and for the six business areas. We are a bit thin on KPIs, but our Ambition to action still works because the totality is meaningful for us.

All Ambition to actions are established, followed up, and maintained in the MIS system. I discuss MIS and business follow-up in more depth later on.

The Ambition to Action Process

Ambition to action is about *translating* strategies into something more concrete, helping us to *execute* our strategic ambitions, choices, and decisions. But Ambition to action is also about helping front-line teams perform and deliver in their daily operations. Finding the right balance between the two is important.

The translation shall help ensure sufficient integration, from strategy to individual goals. At the same time, we must not use so much glue to secure integration that we lose the necessary freedom and flexibility to sense and respond fast. These two purposes often pull in different directions. We believe that we will get *strong* performance if we hit the right balance. But we do not just want strong performance, we also want *sustainable* performance. This is why we try to *activate* our values and leadership principles in our performance management process and not just leave them as nice words in the StatoilHydro book. (See Exhibit 4.7.)

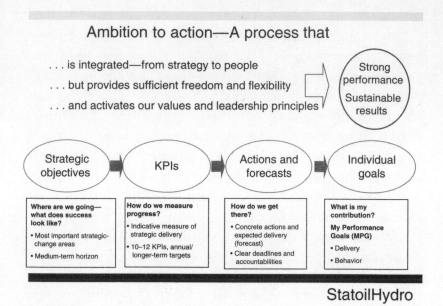

EXHIBIT 4.7 Ambition to Action Principles

We also use Ambition to action to solve what we called the quality problem, the combination of target setting, forecasting, and resource allocation squeezed into one process resulting in one number. These three purposes must first be separated before each one can be improved based on its underlying purpose.

An effective way of separating target setting and forecasting is to separate them in time, which is what we do. (See Exhibit 4.8.) The StatoilHydro merger was actually an example of applying this principle in practice. When the merger was announced in December 2006, it was also said that the new company would be up and running by October 1, 2007. There was no plan at that point showing how this could be done. We were hardly allowed to talk together at the time. The plan came later, driven by this ambitious target. But we made it. If we had done it the other way around, making no start-up commitments before a full master plan was ready, we might still have had an October 1 start-up, but probably it would have occurred a year later.

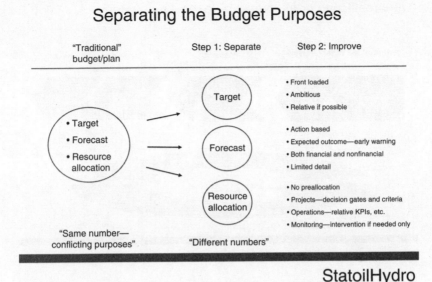

Separating the Budget Purposes

| "Traditional" budget/plan | Step 1: Separate | Step 2: Improve |

Target
- Front loaded
- Ambitious
- Relative if possible

- Target
- Forecast
- Resource allocation

Forecast
- Action based
- Expected outcome—early warning
- Both financial and nonfinancial
- Limited detail

Resource allocation
- No preallocation
- Projects—decision gates and criteria
- Operations—relative KPIs, etc.
- Monitoring—intervention if needed only

"Same number— conflicting purposes"

"Different numbers"

StatoilHydro

EXHIBIT 4.8 Separate and Improve

The Ambition to action process flows as shown in Exhibit 4.9. It is a somewhat busy picture, so let us go through it step by step.

Strategy and Target Setting

STRATEGIC OBJECTIVES The first part of Ambition to action, the strategic objectives, is born in the strategy process and is our strategy map. The strategy process varies somewhat across the company. At group level it is a continuous and issue-driven process, where strategic themes are addressed as needed or at two regular and longer executive committee strategy sessions each year.

Strategic objectives describe what success looks like on a medium-term time horizon. How long this is depends on the rhythm of the actual business. Our oil-trading business has a very different pulse compared to our exploration business. Once

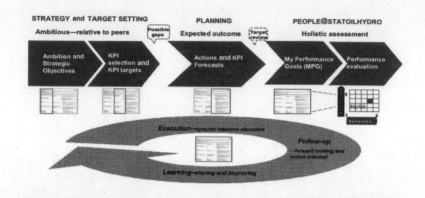

EXHIBIT 4.9 The Ambition to Action Process

established, strategic objectives remain relatively stable unless there are major changes in strategic direction.

Here are some questions we recommend teams to ask when developing and testing the quality of their strategic objectives:

- Do they reflect ambition and strategy; and areas that are both important and need change?
- Do they provide clear guidance and direction?
- Are they written in a language that makes people tick without too many buzzwords?
- Do they support each other (cause and effect, from people and organization to finance)?
- Is the time horizon right, within a relevant delivery period?

The importance of tone and language used is often underestimated. Strategic messages can easily be lost in too many words where "correct and complete" win over "makes people tick." Consulting language is full of words to be avoided, because they do not reach people the way we think they do. Take the popular word "excellence," for example. It is a worn-out expression that turns more people off than on. "World class" is in a similar category. Actually, many people are probably much more fired up by "Let's beat the s*** out of the competition!" I leave it to you to judge if something like that can be said in your own organization. In any case, aim for a simple and natural language, but paint big pictures that engage and that people can relate to and believe in. Think about what kind of language it is that ignites you. Trust your instincts more than the buzzwords. Strategic objectives ideally should be formulated in such a way that people respond with a roaring "Yes, this is a journey I want to be part of!"

Many management teams get impatient when working on strategic objectives. They want to move on to KPIs and actions, which they feel are more concrete and tangible compared to the longer-term strategic objectives. It is, however, critically important to spend sufficient time developing strategic objectives, and it must be done *together*. These discussions, where strategies are sharpened and crystallized, often bring to the table different interpretations of strategic direction that otherwise might have been left unnoticed and unaddressed. Dag Larsson, head of the Swedish consulting company EKAN, puts it like this: "Speed can never replace direction."

It is also much more difficult to define good KPIs if the groundwork is not done on strategic objectives. Remember that the main purpose of a KPI is to measure that we are *moving toward* these objectives. If we jump straight to KPIs without being clear and agreeing on what they measure, how do we know which KPIs to select?

With so many Ambition to actions in the company, we have continuous discussions about the right way and the right order to establish strategic objectives at different levels. Obviously, they have to hang together reasonably well. Some argue for a stringently sequenced process, where no level starts before the level above is finished. Today, this part of the process is quite fluid, with little orchestration from the top. Personally, I am quite comfortable with this. If we had started out as a new company from scratch, maybe some initial structured process would have been necessary. But we are not. Most units are quite familiar with the strategies relevant for them, even if others have not yet finished updating their strategic objectives. If there should be any surprises, we can always adjust later on. The more self-regulating the process is, the better.

What we do not want is a mechanical cascading of identical strategic objectives and, worse, of KPIs and actions. Not all strategies should be born at the top. When they are, the process should be more about strategy *translation*, each level interpreting and translating what objectives from the level above mean for it. In addition, each unit should run its own strategy process as necessary. This might add on themes and objectives that cannot be read out of the messages from above. It can also bring out new strategic issues that might influence strategies above. It is critical for ownership and commitment that units and teams feel they are in the driver's seat and not just passive backseat passengers when their own Ambition to action is developed. This is possible even with clear guidance and direction from above.

From a group perspective, strategic objectives become more and more operational the closer to the front line we get. But that is exactly what we want, to translate the overall strategy into something more concrete and "executionable." The front-line units still see their own more operational objectives as strategic. These objectives provide guidance and direction. We once considered changing the name "strategic objectives" to something more operational in this part of the organization. But where should we switch, and how should we explain it? "You guys should focus on today and forget about direction and tomorrow." I am glad we did not act on that idea.

We recommend focusing Ambition to action on themes that meet *two* criteria: They should of course reflect *important* strategic areas, and these should also be areas where we want *change*. A strategy might address many important areas, but for some of these areas we do not want any change, because the situation is OK. For these, we have other and more suitable places in MIS outside Ambition to action, such as a monitoring section. Here we can monitor the development on "important but OK" issues. If any of these starts showing a negative development and is turning into a problem, we can lift it into Ambition to action with a corresponding action program until the problem is solved.

KEY PERFORMANCE INDICATORS: SELECTION AND TARGET SETTING Earlier we discussed some of the characteristics of a good KPI. Here is the full checklist we use:

- Do they measure progress toward strategic objectives?
- Do they measure real performance (relative; input/output, benchmarks)?
- Is there a good mix of lead and lag indicators (lead: measures input or what creates results; lag: measures output or results)?
- Do they address areas where we want change or improvement (or is monitoring sufficient)?
- Are the KPIs perceived as meaningful at the level they are used?
- Do they have a baseline, and can data be collected easily?

Many people ask about the right number of KPIs on an Ambition to action. There is no right answer, but we generally recommend between 10 and 15.

Relative performance

- Connect input with output

- Compare with others

StatoilHydro

EXHIBIT 4.10 Relative Performance

The most difficult among these guidelines is obviously find-ing good *relative* KPIs, especially to find peers to compare with, inside or outside the company. Most companies are not like Handelsbanken, where internal comparisons between branches and regions are relatively easy. There are, however, several pos-sibilities if we just think slightly outside of the box. Market share percentages can be replaced with market share rankings, pro-duction regularity percentages with internal league standings, and so on. If there is no one else to compare with, you al-ways have the fallback of using yourself and your own past performance as a benchmark.

Exhibit 4.10 is the picture we use to illustrate what we mean by relative KPIs. There are two levels of "relativity." The first is about input/output relations, focusing on unit cost instead of absolute cost; the second is about benchmarking and comparing with others.

The two financial KPIs on the group's Ambition to action are both relative, in the second category. The first one, relative return on capital employed (ROCE), used to be expressed as a percentage number. One year the target was 12%, adjusted for oil price development. The finance function loved such targets. We could accurately report monthly progress. The actual ROCE crept upward as we approached year-end: 11.5%, 11.7%, 11.9% before it just passed 12% at year-end. Great performance! Well, what if the competition delivered returns of 13%, 14%, or 15%?

We have therefore established a league standings list of 14 other reasonably similar oil and gas companies. We compare our own ROCE performance with this peer group. The target is a certain league standings position, and that is not at the bottom. We have done the same with the other financial KPI, relative shareholder return, which is our dividend-adjusted share price development compared to the same peer group. These two KPI targets are the main financial targets the board approves, as part of its overall Ambition to action approval.

We had some concerns when we first communicated these new metrics to the market. Would analysts think we were trying to escape their tough scrutiny, by no longer committing to concrete return targets? The analysts hardly blinked. Why? Because this is what they do all the time: compare the performance of one oil company to that of other oil companies. They probably rank us on more parameters than we do ourselves!

These relative financial targets are not cascaded mathematically to business areas, as doing so is not meaningful or possible. They are instead translated in various ways. One business area has defined its main financial target as having "ROCE at group level." Others have simply taken the corporate relative ROCE target as their own, as a measure of shared success. Others have no overall profitability targets at all. But if they deliver on their Ambition to action, they will most likely produce outstanding financial results.

We are currently working together with the health, safety, and environment (HSE) function in making some of its KPIs relative. We have an impressive number of KPIs in this area. A common one is "serious incident frequency," which measures the number of serious incidents per million man-hours worked. Targets are set annually in a large number of units. Although the target-setting process is quite lean, too much time is still spent on negotiating target levels, involving both managers and support staff. It is a "decimal" discussion. Let us assume the current performance in a unit is 3.2. The manager would typically expect that performance should improve further, and that next year's target ought to be 3.0. The response would be a long list of arguments why simply holding the fort at 3.2 is more than challenging enough. After weeks of discussion and negotiation, they end up where everybody knew they would: at 3.1.

We want to stop all of this. We want units to establish (or be placed in) a league standings list of similar units. The target would be set once, with no need for annual changes. It could be to *advance* in the league standings, be *above average*, or similar. By doing this we believe we will achieve several things. First, there is no need to negotiate targets every year. These are evergreen targets. Second, with *above average*, managers would be taking on a quite ambitious target without protests. Half of the peer group would on average not make it, but few would still see it as too ambitious. Who would openly aim for below average? And last but not least, those coming out low might become more interested in learning from those above.

We constantly discuss how ambitious our targets should be. We often quote Aristotle. (See Exhibit 4.11.) We do this because many people tend to forget the *purpose* of goals and targets. The purpose is to motivate and drive, to secure the best possible performance even when this turns out to be lower than targeted. What is best performance (if high is good): delivering

Our problem is not that we aim too high and miss, but that we aim too low and hit.

— Aristotle

StatoilHydro

EXHIBIT 4.11 Aristotle on Target Setting

100 against a target of 100, or delivering 105 against a target of 110?

Most would agree that there has to be a certain element of stretch in a target. The issue is how much. There is no simple answer. The more ambitious a target is, the less it must be perceived as imposed from above. Without ownership and commitment, ambitious targets become nothing but a numbers game. Unfortunately, the market and the external world do not always seem to appreciate this way of looking at performance and targets. The consequence is that we need to separate external and internal targets. The market seems to appreciate "aim low and hit" more than not fully meeting a demanding stretch target. It may not be the intention, but that is often the consequence of the market's focus on hitting the numbers. Sometimes it even seems like performance is about hitting the analysts' consensus expectation, because they do not like "surprises." There are companies that have left this game, that give no promises, no guiding, and hold no "capital market day." We all know getting there can be achieved only through consistently delivering good performance. The catch-22 is that the singing and dancing around quarterly results and short-term targets might actually prevent companies from reaching the performance levels required to quit the game.

Let us close this section with a few words on target-setting frequency and time horizons. Our group, business area, and business unit level strategic objectives and KPIs are reviewed and adjusted as needed in the spring. When this job is finalized, KPI targets are set as described, some before and some after the summer. The key point is to set direction and finalize target setting *before* moving into the planning phase in the autumn. KPI targets are set for the coming year and for longer periods where relevant, such as for production. On some KPIs we have introduced rolling three-year averages. This is typically done where the business has a longer-term nature—exploration, for example. It takes several years to secure access to an area, shoot and interpret seismic, plan, drill, and analyze the results. One-year periods and targets do not make sense here. In the "What's next?" section you can read more about our ideas about a much less calendar-driven process.

Planning: Actions and Forecasts

When we know what we are aiming for and where we are going, it is time to plan how to get there. Planning is about *two things only*:

1. Which *actions* do we need to take in order to deliver on strategic objectives and KPI targets?
2. What are the expected consequences of our actions, expressed as a *forecast*, either against KPI targets or on other

financial or operational areas without targets, but where we need to understand what lies ahead (such as financial capacity)?

Planning is not about target setting, because this lies behind us. Neither is it about resource allocation, because this is handled in a separate process.

Actions need to be ambitious, because what we aim for is challenging. The consequence of these actions, the forecast, must, however, reflect the *expected outcome*, whether we like what we see or not. The forecast shall reveal issues on the radar screen early enough for us to take the necessary corrective actions.

Because targets must be ambitious and forecasts realistic, it is quite natural to have *gaps* between the two. The purpose is of course to close such gaps, as deadlines and delivery time are approaching. A gap is nothing negative; it just shows that we are able to have two thoughts in our heads at the same time. It confirms that we are aiming high while at the same time we have a realistic view on where we believe we will end up as things look today. Having no gaps sometimes is more questionable, especially if delivery time is some time ahead. This might indicate ambitions that are too low or forecasts that are too optimistic.

Yet if targets become too ambitious, gaps can become too big. This can be dangerous, because it can lead to outcomes we do not want. People might give up or do stupid things to deliver. We have therefore established a "target review" mechanism. This is an opportunity to have targets adjusted if gaps turn out to be too tough to close. It is not used very often, but the organization knows it exist and knows it is for real. In the last couple of years, a few business areas have asked for adjustments on a few KPI targets. But normally units stick with their targets even when gaps seem challenging to close.

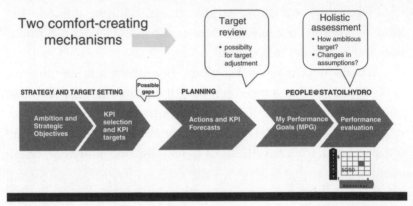

EXHIBIT 4.12 Comfort Mechanisms

Setting targets before doing the planning can be uncomfortable, and even more so if targets also are expected to be
ambitious. (See Exhibit 4.12.) We therefore need mechanisms
that can create *comfort*. The target review is one such mechanism. Another one is the holistic performance evaluation, where
stretching is rewarded and not punished, and where changes in
assumptions might be taken into account. This is further explained in the "Performance Evaluation and Rewards" section.

A target adjustment can lead only to less ambitious targets,
not the opposite. If people know that a forecast showing performance better than target will lead to tougher targets, this
might be the last time we would see such a positive gap. People would quickly learn the consequence, and some might be
tempted, consciously or unconsciously, to adjust their forecast
accordingly. We need those realistic forecasts, when they pre-
dict delivery better than target as well as the reverse.

The forecast is not a do-nothing base case. It includes expected consequences of new actions. If the forecast is based on ambitious actions and initiatives, the probability of success will be less than 100% for each of them, and an appropriate weighting is therefore done.

The theory is simple, but the practice is not, for several reasons. The first has to do with our heritage from the budget days, which are not that far behind us. In the old process, there was "one number" only. This was optimized depending on the main purpose: a "high" number if the main purpose was to ask for money and a "low" number if the main purpose was target negotiation.

Now, a forecast should just be a forecast and nothing else. If you game your forecast, the only one you fool in the end is yourself. Even if most people understand and appreciate the difference, we still see skewed forecasts. As we learned about investment forecasting in Borealis, it takes time to leave old behaviors behind, much longer than we think. Unconsciously, many managers still let their forecast sway in the direction that would have paid off in the old system. We are seeing less and less of this, but it still happens.

Another distortion effect comes from the fear of bringing bad news. If there are clouds on the horizon, it is tempting to hope they will disappear and not cause stormy weather. The one to blame is often the forecast receiver. Reactions to bad news are seldom positive. "Why didn't you see this coming much earlier?" "Why haven't you planned for this?" or "I want your updated action plan by tomorrow." Who wants to bring bad news if these are the responses? Remember, the forecasts that we do not like often are the most useful ones. They enable us to take action early enough to avoid hitting the outcomes we do not like. (See Exhibit 4.13.)

What I am talking about here is *bias* in forecasting, conscious or unconscious. It is a systematic error. Bias is different

The purpose of forecasting

Get issues on the radar
screen early enough . . .

. . . to enable corrective
actions

Brutally honest—actionable—right time horizon—right detail level

StatoilHydro

EXHIBIT 4.13 Forecasting

from *noise.* Noise is random variations above and below the actual outcome, with no systematic patterns. Noise is inevitable, and we need to understand the difference between the two when analyzing how good we are on our forecasting.

A forecast is *not* a promise, not something to "deliver on." People using that expression have not understood the difference between a forecast and a target. A forecast is what we *think* will happen; a target is what we *want to* happen. A forecast reflects the expected outcome, desirable or not. Sometimes we do not want to hit our forecasts. If we do not like what we see, we initiate corrective actions to adjust the course, to *avoid* hitting that forecast. After a while we make a new forecast, checking the effect of ongoing actions, taking into account new information and changes in assumptions.

Making a good forecast is a science in itself. In accounting, we have thick manuals, well-documented procedures, and detailed audits to check the quality. In forecasting, we have next to nothing. An exception in our industry is the practice we find in construction projects, where a continuous update of the "master control estimate" is a profession in itself. But also here we see the occasional gaming: the reluctance to lower cost estimates because it is perceived as giving back money that might be needed for a rainy day and that might have to be "asked" for again later. In other words, forecasting is mixed up with resource allocation.

It is important to have correct and reliable accounting information. But it is just as important to have high forecasting quality. This information is the main basis for making decisions about new projects, new initiatives, and corrective actions, the value-creating activities that later end up as profit, which we accurately can account for in the books. Forecasting is actually "accounting on the future" instead of on the past (of course not with the same "one right answer" and detail level). Forecasting as the basis for decision making is *more* important than accounting when it comes to creating *new* value, not just tapping value from earlier decisions and the existing portfolio. Also these assets were once new decisions, made based on forecasts about what then was ahead of us and now is behind us as actual numbers in the accounts.

We must not, however, turn forecasting into a new accounting industry. Not everything should be forecasted. Many parameters carry so much uncertainty that they cannot be predicted in a meaningful way. Oil prices and exchange rates are probably in this category. When I worked in Statoil's crude oil marketing unit, there was an impressive knowledge on the fundamentals of oil markets and the mechanisms that drives oil prices. Still, I am not sure if the average prediction hit rate on both short- and long-term price movements was very different from what a rolling dice would have done. Of course, we need to make assumptions on oil price and other important parameters, but multiple scenarios, ranges, and what-if analyses might be more meaningful than one number only.

Here are a few simple but important forecasting principles. Forecasting is primarily something *you do for yourself*. If a lot of your forecasting is triggered by requests from above, asking for data you otherwise would not have bothered with to manage your own business, then something is wrong. Why do "they" need this information if you do not? There will of course be exceptions, but generally this principle should apply. Levels above can tap into your data for their more consolidated forecasts. This ownership is also key for getting good data quality. You always get better quality if those providing the data also depend on the quality themselves.

A forecast should also be *actionable*. If the information cannot be used to trigger any corrective action, why do we forecast? Often requests from above seem to be automatic: "We have always asked for this." Such requests often come without any explanation of the underlying reason why the information is needed; which would have been very helpful to the ones being asked. Then they might respond: "If this is what you're after, you should ask for this and not for that. And you already got some slightly different numbers last week that are good enough for this purpose. Next time maybe you can make a rough calculation yourself, instead of collecting and adding up data from a lot of units below." It is also important that people ask: "What is the purpose of this forecast? What kind of corrective actions will you be able to take with this information?" It is amazing how much forecasting takes place where these simple questions are not asked or cannot be answered very convincingly. The unnecessary requests often come from finance people who lack sufficient front-line business knowledge, who are too afraid to stick their necks out and make a roughly right estimate themselves. Rotating people between the front line and central staffs is an effective way to change this kind of behavior. The other source for unnecessary forecasting is of course requests from "control" managers who ask for much more than they need, understand, or can do anything about.

Relative KPIs and forecasting require a few comments. A relative KPI measures your own performance against that of someone else. You might be able to forecast your own expected performance, but it is much harder to forecast how others will perform. Is this a problem? Not necessarily. It simply means that the main focus must be on performing as well as you possibly can, and you might forecast just that if relevant. From time to time you get competitor data that says something about how you are doing. If you are lagging behind, you will probably make an extra effort. And that is what we want. The goal is good performance; a forecast is just something to help achieve that.

Some of you might have waited for a description of a rolling forecast process in Statoil. In fact, we did not implement one. The initial reason for not taking this step was simply that it would be too much on top of everything else when we started out in 2005. We were waiting for a natural opportunity to launch this part. And we are glad we waited. We now see that this perhaps is *not* the right next step for us. Read more about this at the end of the Statoil case.

People@StatoilHydro Part 1

MY PERFORMANCE GOALS   Ambition to action defines, directly or indirectly, the delivery goals in "My Performance Goals" (MPGs), which are established for all employees in the company. (See Exhibit 4.14.) When a management team *together* has finalized an Ambition to action, they have also defined the *delivery* goals for the manager and also for most of the team. There is no second, private negotiation leading to a set of different delivery goals, as often was the case before. Such a double set of delivery goals can completely undermine the credibility of Ambition

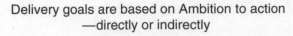

Delivery goals are based on Ambition to action
—directly or indirectly

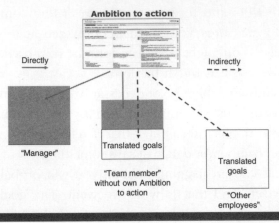

StatoilHydro

EXHIBIT 4.14 Delivery Goals in the MPG

to action, even if the actual differences are small. What kind of
motivation and commitment does a manager create when rally-
ing the team around common team goals in Ambition to action,
while everybody knows there is a private and secret piece of
paper in the back pocket that says something else? If a bonus
is involved, the situation is even worse. Again, *transparency*
is key.

If you are a member of a management team with an Ambition to action and do not have your own, your delivery goals
are sourced from that Ambition to action. Some strategic objectives, KPI targets, or actions are copied directly; others are
translated and personalized. For those farther away from an Ambition to action, there is less direct copying and more personal
translation.

MPGs are not just about *what* to deliver. They are also
about expectations on *how* delivery shall take place. These are

expressed as *behavior* goals. The main purpose of behavior goals is to ensure that values and leadership principles are alive and applied when delivering on Ambition to action. Behavior goals are based on the values most critical to Ambition to action delivery, with emphasis on those with the largest improvement potential. If a team is facing a major change, behavior goals might, for instance, address involvement, communication, and motivation. What we want is to *activate* our values and leadership principles in the performance management process. They are all far too important to be left as well-intended words only in the StatoilHydro book.

Not everyone fully understands the reason for the strong emphasis on values; they believe it is all about more "hugging and kissing." I do not mind at all, that would be great! But this is not the purpose of the value focus, which is based on a solid business reason. We must be serious also on this dimension if we aim to deliver *sustainable* results, which hold not only tomorrow but also farther into the future. If we want to keep our license to operate in an environment with increasingly higher expectations, then we cannot ignore values and behavior. Delivery and behavior are therefore weighted 50/50. That decision came directly from CEO Helge Lund. His message was clear: Two things can break the back of the company: a serious integrity violation or a serious accident. The list of companies that are no longer with us due to integrity violations is much longer than the list of those disappearing due to accidents.

Individual goals are mostly set on an annual basis, followed up in a midyear review and evaluated at the end of the year. Breaking out of the calendar year also here is something we discuss in Chapter 5, as well as some second thoughts about team versus individual goals. I also describe how we evaluate performance against delivery and behavior goals through the holistic assessment.

Dynamic Resource Allocation

Newcomers to the model constantly ask: "How on earth can costs be managed without a budget?" It is a natural question, because cost control is what most people see as the main purpose of a budget. Let us first agree on what we really are after. As mentioned earlier, we want an efficient and responsible use of resources, helping us to maximize value creation. It is as simple and as difficult as that. This can *never* be achieved unless there is a foundation of strong values and a responsible mind-set. The question must therefore be answered in two steps. We need to start with the *mind-set* required before we look at *tools and processes* required. No tool or process alone can do this job for us. Exhibit 4.15 illustrates what we want to leave and how we would like people to think instead.

The mind-set we want to move away from is the one expressed by "Do I have a budget for this?" as the main question

Dynamic resource allocation:
A different mindset—cost conscious from the first penny

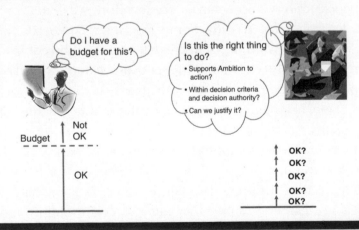

StatoilHydro

EXHIBIT 4.15 A Different Mind-Set

asked when a decision with cost implications must be made. The answer is normally *yes* if there is budget money available; otherwise it is *no*.

We want instead people to ask "Is this the right thing to do? Is this something that supports our Ambition to action? Is this something I can justify?" If in doubt, a good test is to think ahead and imagine that the answer was *yes* and the money has been spent. Afterward, a colleague or a manager comes over and questions whether this was a wise decision. If the decision is uncomfortable to stand up and defend, then maybe one should think twice or discuss it with someone first. Our ethics policy recommends the same kind of test when facing ethical dilemmas.

In addition, we must, of course, ensure that a decision is within our decision criteria and decision authorities (most relevant for larger projects and major new activities) and that we have the financial and organizational capacity. The financial capacity comes out of our financial forecasting. The organizational capacity we still struggle with, like most other companies, as we discussed in the "Cost Management Problem" section in Chapter 1.

The right mind-set is *necessary* but not *sufficient* for an efficient resource allocation process. We are not naive. We do not believe costs in Scandinavia's largest company can be managed by the right mind-set only. A bit more is needed. We have therefore established a toolbox of alternative mechanisms, as illustrated in Exhibit 4.16. What we want is a dynamic allocation of resources that is as *self-regulating* as possible. We have a menu of alternatives to achieve just that. Starting from left, the options are:

- A traditional cost budget is a total cost number with a detailed split. It provides very limited freedom and flexibility.

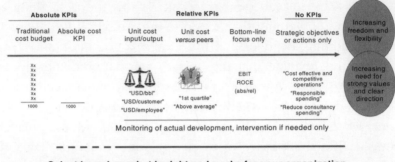

Dynamic resource allocation—alternative approaches

Monitoring of actual development, intervention if needed only

Select based on what is right and works for your organization

StatoilHyddro

EXHIBIT 4.16 Dynamic Resource Allocation

- Dropping the details and giving freedom within the total number is a step in the right direction, but many of the budget problems remain unsolved. If there is a lot of uncertainty ahead, how do we know that 1000 is the right number? Why not 900 or 1100?

- A further step is to move from absolute to relative measurement. A unit cost target is more flexible than an absolute number. The higher the output, the more can be spent on input, and vice versa. It is a self-regulating mechanism.

- Focusing instead on our own unit cost compared to others through a targeted league standings position creates additional flexibility. It also neutralizes changes in assumptions that affect all players in the league, such as changes in demand or in raw material prices.

- It is also possible to operate without any cost KPIs at all and instead rely on the self-regulating effect of a challenging bottom-line target, such as operating profit or ROCE, absolute or relative. You cannot spend more unless you get more back. If this is the case, we talk about good costs, and those are quite OK.

- Finally, it is possible to manage costs without any KPI targets at all. Instead we rely on the two other dimensions in Ambition to action. Strategic objectives can express what kind of cost mentality we want, such as "No waste in our team" or "We spend company money as carefully as our own money." Actions can be more concrete: "Fewer suppliers," "Reduced use of consultants," "Less travel, more telephone conferences." All of this can, of course, be said in combination with some of the direct or indirect KPIs already discussed.

This is a menu, without one right answer about where a unit should be. It depends on the type of business and where the team is on its own journey. Several of the options can also be used in combination. All of them assume, of course, that the financial or organizational capacity is in place. If it is not, targets or mandates could be adjusted or more projects could be turned down.

The model is based on trust, on the belief that the majority of people are mature and can be trusted to spend money wisely. The farther to the right we move, the more trust we show and the more dependent we are on a solid value foundation and on the fact that that the strategy is understood and embraced. A project could be on the left, with a fixed cost estimate, without necessarily representing a lack of trust. This left part of the menu is, however, seldom recommended for running operations.

The staff unit I am based in has not had a budget for many years. We have not found any meaningful cost KPIs, so we are operating on the far-right end of the scale. But our costs are not exploding. We actually find it *more* difficult to spend money without a budget. With an approved budget, you often spend without too much concern until you start seeing the bottom of the bag. Without a budget, there is a much higher awareness around the question "Is this the right thing to do?" and you get it on *all* spending, from the first penny. Another interesting effect is what happens when someone shows you trust. In our team, everyone wants to prove that we deserve to be trusted, that we are up to it. It is about earning the right to be trusted.

But even if we trust, we are not naive. The minority, those who are either too smart or too immature to handle trust, is a reality we must face and relate to. "Behind the curtain" we therefore monitor actual trends and developments, using both accounting and forecasting data. If trends look OK, we do nothing. Why should we? If trends start to look a bit strange, we ask the necessary questions. Almost always, we get sound and good business justifications. But there will also be cases where our questions reveal the opposite: managers who unconsciously have lost focus on cost or, worse, consciously misused the freedom they got. In these cases, we have *not* abdicated the right to intervene and to manage in the old way when necessary. These managers can be moved immediately to the far left of the menu and given an old-fashioned budget, if they still should continue in their jobs.

Let us look at an example of these principles applied in practice by revisiting Global Exploration, as shown in Exhibit 4.17. This exhibit, from this unit's Ambition to action, first highlights two KPIs that are relevant from a resource allocation perspective (all numbers illustrative):

1. *Access cost* is a unit cost KPI, measuring what it costs, on average, to find a new barrel of oil. It is measured as a three-year average, because one year is too short in this long-term business. The target is inspired both by own previous performance and by competitors' performance.

Dynamic resource allocation—an example

Mechanism	Global Exploration
KPI targets	• Access cost max 4 USD/barrel (3 yrs avg) • New resources 200 million barrels (3 yrs avg)
Decision authorities	• $50 million USD • New country/partner
Decision gates and criteria	• Expected Net Present Value min x million USD • Probability of drilling success min xx% • Plus others
Monitoring	• Monitoring of actual trends and development • Intervention only if needed

(Illustrative numbers)

Spending expected to be within direction of Ambition to action

StatoilHydro

EXHIBIT 4.17 Dynamic Resource Allocation Example

2. *New resources* measures how much of new oil and gas reserves Global Exploration discovers. The target is driven by the company's growth ambitions and also is a three-year average.

If we multiply these two target numbers, we get $800 million. This is, however, *not* a budget. Global Exploration can spend more if it finds more within the access cost target and is expected to spend less if it finds less. It is a not a fixed and preallocated amount but a *dynamic and self-regulating* process. Again, how can we know up front exactly what the right spending level should be, with all the uncertainty about new opportunities, rig markets, drilling progress, and so on?

In addition, all exploration decisions taken by the management team itself must be within established decision authorities, which is the second lever that replaces budgets. Finally, all larger decisions are pressure tested by the Exploration Arena, an independent body that calls on relevant competence from across the company to assist in structured project reviews as projects pass predefined decisions gates. These reviews address projects from many angle: technical, HSE, finance, HR, political risk, and so on. The arena has no decision authority, but few seek final decision gate approval of their project with a negative arena recommendation. Similar arenas also exist for field development projects and for information technology (IT) projects.

What if the oil price falls, times get tougher, and we need to spend less money on exploration? First of all, this area should never be the place to start. Exploration is the seed corn for an oil company. But if we have to, the old way was at least simple: We would just cut exploration budgets by the necessary percentage. Now we would start with lowering the "new resources" target because we cannot afford such high ambitions. If this is not enough, we might move to "access cost" and reduce the targeted cost per barrel. If this still is insufficient, we might raise the profitability criteria so that only the very best projects pass. Finally, we might have to tell Global Exploration that even if we still trust the unit, money is now so tight that we need to lift more of its project decisions one level up to calibrate them against other business opportunities.

Let us close this section with what Beyond Budgeting means for larger projects. I have always been puzzled by the paradox that we decide on these projects using criteria that we leave behind once we move into execution and follow-up. Projects typically are analyzed and decided with value creation and net present value as the key financial criteria. Afterward, the focus narrows. Targets and follow-up are now all about *time* and *cost*. The consequence is often no room for good costs or more time, even when this would have increased the value of the project.

In Statoil's history, the value creation and do-the-right-thing focus during project execution has been winning over the fixed budget from time to time. Unfortunately, media and the external world seem to understand time and cost, and little else. The price paid in company reputation and individual careers has been high.

Even if projects typically are on the left side of the menu, the annual allocation is gone. There is no longer an annual investment budget. Projects are approved as they come, but they do not come without a warning. We have a quarterly updated investment forecast, which of course includes projects in the pipeline that are not yet approved. In addition, there is often a generic part farther out in time, representing projects we know will come but do not yet have a name. In our "international" long-term forecasts, the generic part is substantial. A significant part of the future capital spending in this part of the business is acquisition projects not yet on the radar screen of either buyer or seller.

The arena evaluation process is also important, taking larger projects through a structured pressure-testing at defined maturity stages. This is another example of existing processes already doing what the budget aims for, but in a much better way. Here a continuous investment forecast is combined with an effective decision-making process on individual projects.

What about portfolio optimization and project prioritization? This takes place continuously based on the as-late-as-possible principle. We will never have perfect information available to make the optimal trade-offs between projects, but the longer we can wait, the better information we have (while of course taking "waiting costs" into account). Although not a waterproof concept, this approach will anyhow be better than trying to do it all in an annual budget stint.

Back to the individual investment project. As in the quality problem, the conflict between targets, forecasts, and resource allocation is just as relevant for projects. Therefore, we no longer have only *one* single project number approved. Instead, we now operate with three numbers:

1. The forecast, the *project estimate*, which is the expected cost estimate used in the profitability analysis and approval of the project
2. A lower and more ambitious *target cost* number, which is the cost level the project team tries to deliver on
3. A higher *resource allocation estimate*, which is set higher than the project estimate (which by definition has a 50% chance of ending higher), to avoid every second project having to come back and ask for more money

As a consequence, the phrase "project budget" is slowly disappearing from investment projects as well, because it no longer is a meaningful term to use. It is happening slowly, because the word "budget" is a difficult one for many people to leave behind.

Business Follow-Up

Business follow-up is built around monthly reporting and review meetings against Ambition to action. Many business reviews are done live in the MIS system, supported by other information only where necessary. In addition, a short weekly status report is made, also in MIS, built from business unit level. A key principle in our business follow-up is "forward looking and action oriented." The KPI status (red/yellow/green) is therefore set by comparing *forecasts* with year-end *targets*, instead of actual versus budget year to date. The purpose is to shift the focus forward, away from the past and on explaining historical deviations. This does not mean that we do not understand our actual figures. It is the comparison to an increasingly outdated reference point that we are skipping.

The business reviews focus not only on KPI status but on the whole Ambition to action. The strategic objectives stand there as a constant reminder of what we are aiming for longer term. They are something against which KPI results and actions must be calibrated constantly. Actions are also color-coded. The color is driven by whether the action is expected to deliver the planned outcome. Actions are managed dynamically in the system. Completed ones are closed, ongoing ones are monitored, and new ones are established as necessary. All of this is done by the team owning the Ambition to action, not by any central staff.

Two key questions triggered by the KPI status are:

1. If the KPI is green, which risks can jeopardize this expected development, and how are these risks addressed?
2. If the KPI is red, which actions are initiated to get back on track?

Where relevant, the KPI status is reported in rolling windows, typically covering 13 or 15 months. The purpose is to provide better trend reporting than what you get in a January–December picture, which on average always is half empty. Compare the graphs in Exhibits 4.18 and 4.19. Which provides better information?

People@StatoilHydro Part 2

PERFORMANCE EVALUATION AND REWARDS A key purpose of Ambition to action is to provide a broader and better language for describing and evaluating performance. The old language was quite simple. Good performance was about delivering on budget numbers. Then we introduced scorecards and got a new phrase in the performance vocabulary: "green or red KPI." When we dropped budgets, we were again left with one word only, this time the KPI color.

Ambition to action has given us a new and more holistic performance language, with more words available. This

Turning the reporting focus, from history to future...

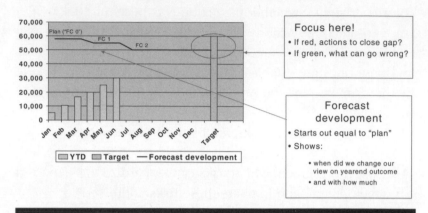

EXHIBIT 4.18 Report Example 1

. . . and moving to rolling reporting where possible

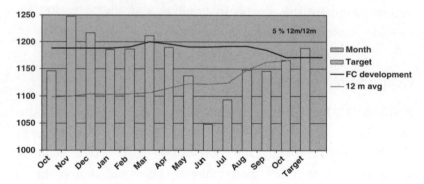

EXHIBIT 4.19 Report Example 2

broadening has taken place in two dimensions. First, delivery is no longer based on KPIs only but on the whole Ambition to action, supported by a structured assessment of delivered results. Second, the introduction of behavior provided us with a completely new dimension in our performance language.

Delivery goals are evaluated through a *pressure-testing* of delivered results, initially measured as KPI results against KPI targets. These KPI results are now only the *starting point* for an evaluation, not the end point, because a KPI is only an *indicator*. These five questions are used to pressure test the KPI results:

1. **Did delivered results contribute toward the strategic objectives?** If we take off our KPI glasses and look at what the KPI was unable to pick up, how does it look? There is normally a lot of hindsight information available. The answer might confirm what the KPI indicated or reveal a more positive or negative picture.
2. **How ambitious were the targets?** Did you stretch yourself? This is often much more visible afterward than when the target was established. The answer can give credit for aiming high compared to others with equal delivery but who were successful in talking down their target commitments.
3. **Are there changes in assumptions that should be taken into account?** Did you have tailwind or headwind that had nothing to do with your own performance?
4. **Were agreed or necessary actions taken?** Did you continuously establish and execute new corrective actions as needed?
5. **Are the results sustainable?** Or has there been suboptimization in order to lift short-term results?

These questions are not asked for each KPI but for each of the five perspectives. The intention with these questions is not

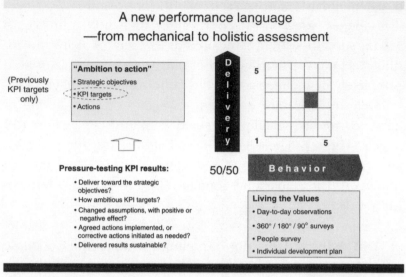

StatoilHydro

EXHIBIT 4.20 A New Performance Language

to create a long list of excuses for nondelivery; the purpose is to understand and agree on relevant background information and then conclude on how much of this should be taken into account. (See Exhibit 4.20.)

There are several information sources available for establishing and evaluating *behavior* goals. These include the Even Stronger survey, which gives 360-, 180-, or 90-degree feedback on how managers and employees are living the values. Another source is the organizational climate survey, where some questions provide direct feedback to individual managers. It is important to remember that these survey data are indications only. We must not end up with the same KPI-dominated evaluation as we used to have on business results. Day-to-day observations and sound judgment are therefore necessary supplements. Many of the pressure-testing questions are also applicable when evaluating behavior goals. It is not easy to set and evaluate behavior goals, and we are learning every day. But we are convinced that this is the right thing to do. Things were not easy when we started with KPIs many years ago either.

The outcome of the delivery and behavior evaluation results in a score on a 1-to-5 scale in each dimension. The resulting position in the evaluation matrix is used both for next year's individual development plan, for base salary increases, and for individual bonuses. So far Statoil has been quite modest on both reach and size of individual bonuses. We have also broken the fixed performance contract, the mechanical link between targets and reward, by introducing the holistic performance evaluation. The bonus area is one of the few remaining areas where we follow mainstream performance management. As I have mentioned, I am highly skeptical regarding the motivational effect of the individual bonus. There were a lot of great performances and outstanding achievements in the company in the many years before individual bonuses were introduced in 1998. The conditions created and levers pulled at that time prior to the introduction of bonuses are things bonus believers should try to understand better before pushing for further increases in bonus size and coverage.

On the positive side, there is also a collective bonus scheme for all employees, based on how the company is doing compared to the competition on the two corporate KPIs: relative ROCE and relative shareholder return. In addition, there is a very popular share savings program, where all employees can buy shares for up to 5% of their base salary each year and receive one free share for each one bought. Shares must be kept for a minimum of two years.

In 2008 it was decided to split the collective bonus in two, with up to 5% on the group level and up to 5% on business area performance. I am quite skeptical about this. We have chosen an organizational model in which interdependence and the need for cooperation between business areas are higher than ever. I do not think the change in the bonus structure will support such cooperation; on the contrary. The negative effect might not be very big, but it pulls in the wrong direction. Such schemes are (rightly) about indirectly motivating by sharing common success rather than creating up-front individual motivation. By differentiating between business areas like this when interdependencies are so high, I am convinced that the collective motivation will suffer. We will make more people unhappy than happy. It will create more dissatisfaction and negative discussions among those coming in low than it will create positive reactions from those coming in high.

Scorecard Pitfalls

In both Borealis and Statoil, scorecards were high on the list of tools and processes that replaced the budget. I like the balanced scorecard concept, because it is very much based on common sense. It helps us to connect: long term and short term, cause and effect, financial and nonfinancial, line and support, strategy, finance, and HR. It provides us with a better performance language than perhaps any other management concept has been able to do.

One reason for the huge popularity of scorecards is the impressive packaging and marketing of the concept. Nevertheless, behind all that nice wrapping lies a solid concept. However, if the balanced scorecard is implemented in the wrong way, its full potential will not be realized. In the worst case, scorecards can do even more damage than budgets. In this section we look at some typical pitfalls. There are enough balanced scorecard success stories out there; I believe there is more to learn by understanding where things can go wrong. What I discuss next is all based on experiences from my first encounter with scorecards in Borealis back in 1995.

There are many ways of getting it wrong. I list here seven classic mistakes. There are probably more to watch out for. Some are more dangerous than others, especially the command-and-control one. In combination, they are almost guaranteed to make you fail. None of these pitfalls should be read as an argument against the balanced scorecard. On the contrary, I point them out in order to help you get the maximum benefit out of the concept.

The pitfalls are:

1. A new box on top of old boxes.
2. It is all about KPIs.
3. Just another command-and-control tool.
4. Only one scorecard at the top.
5. A paralyzing balance.
6. It is a finance thing.
7. It is a manual thing.

A New Box on Top of Old Boxes

I have often wondered where the consulting world stands on Beyond Budgeting. After Borealis and other cases, after the Beyond Budgeting book by Robin Fraser and Jeremy Hope and the Beyond Budgeting Round Table, I had expected the consulting business to grab the idea, wrap it and market it as "the next big thing," and of course charge accordingly. For some reason, this has not happened, at least not yet. There are indications that something might be brewing, but that will be late as the budget criticism and the Beyond Budgeting movement has been with us for a long time now. Is it because Beyond Budgeting is too big? Is it too provocative? Is it challenging too many accepted truths? Is it too difficult to box and wrap? Is it the combination of management process and leadership philosophy that confuses? Perhaps the consulting companies have organized management and leadership under separate responsibilities, as it typically would be with their customers?

I am convinced that one day the consulting business will wake up, and with some hesitation I hope they do. I believe we need their muscles and their marketing channels to reach the many top management teams that seem to trust new ideas only when they come from consultants with their impressive presentations. So I welcome consultants to Beyond Budgeting. We must, however, help them understand and embrace the full depth of the idea, so they do not reduce it to a narrow and mechanical concept when their fancy slide show is rolling in front of nodding executives.

But getting consulting help does not guarantee success. One reason why the consulting medicine often fails is that it is so much easier to add on than it is to take away. You can implement a lot of today's highly acclaimed management concepts without really having to threaten the stuff that already exists in the company or those responsible for it. You buy a new box and just put it on top of your other boxes.

Look at the huge number of companies that have implemented balanced scorecards. It has almost become politically incorrect to be without one, especially for larger companies. Almost all of these companies, however, have added the scorecard on top of existing management models, including existing budgeting and planning. It looks nice. No threats, no conflicts. Everybody is happy, beyond those who worry that there is even more to do.

But budgets and scorecards represent two fundamentally different approaches. Scorecards are rooted in strategy and in longer time perspectives. They focus on the nonfinancial drivers that lead to financial performance, all the way back to learning and growth. Budgets are very much the opposite: They have weak strategy links and short time horizons, and are finance oriented. Remember that the balanced scorecard was created as a response to the narrow, financial-only focus that dominated business management for decades.

Many argue that scorecards and budgets is an uncomplicated marriage. They claim that budget numbers and budget follow-up can fill the financial perspective in the scorecard. The other perspectives are established and operated as the theory prescribes, defining and measuring the nonfinancial levers to pull in order to deliver on the budget numbers in the financial perspective. It looks like a good start. It all hangs together, from finance to people. There are, however, major challenges ahead. First, defining good financial performance through fixed and absolute budget numbers is not very smart, for reasons already discussed at length. If you were not moved by those arguments, there is a second problem. You have designed good objectives, KPIs, and actions; and cause-and-effect relations describing how they all link and support each other; and ultimately the financial targets. If your scorecard works well, it will quickly pick up internal or external radar signals when assumptions change and the unexpected happen. The right response often is to adjust the course. Revised tactics and new actions are quickly put in place. People are ready to move, but there is a ball and chain around their legs: *the budget.* To secure delivery of the fixed budget number in the financial perspective, it was cascaded down into every single unit with rigorous detail, spelling out not just profitability targets or the like but also which activities to execute at which cost. The conflict between scorecard and budget is suddenly real and tangible. And the winner is . . .

These two opposites collide more often than we think. When they do, the budget wins, again and again. The budget is familiar, it has a track record, and it often carries the bonus money. Going with the budget is just as safe as selecting SAP as your enterprise system. Nobody is fired for staying within budget. No wonder the scorecard so often loses out, even if everyone thinks it is great. So we keep playing the scorecard game. We cannot drop it, even when we feel it does not work as promised. Everyone else has scorecards.

The answer is not to drop scorecards but to drop the competition: the budget. We never got this insight in Borealis, because we never experienced the competition between the two. We dropped the budget and introduced scorecards in one big bang.

Statoil, however, had been running scorecards in parallel with budgets since 1997, with only reasonable success compared to where the company is today. Removing the budget in 2005 was like turbocharging the entire scorecard process. It soon became clear to the organization that the rules of the game and what would now drive decisions and actions had changed. Now it was all about Ambition to action. The fact that the board no longer approved budgets but only Ambition to action was tangible evidence of a new focus.

I have had many questions from companies considering introducing scorecards and dropping budgets: Should we run in parallel, to get familiar with scorecards before leaving the budgets? Or is it better to go for the big bang? I have tried both methods. The answer depends on your own case for change. If there is a strong pull for change, a big bang is very powerful. The change is immediate and very visible. If the sentiment is more toward "prove that we have a problem and that there is a better way," a parallel approach might be better. On balance, I believe that a parallel implementation is preferable. You might find some further guidance on this question in the next chapter.

It Is All about KPIs

A balanced scorecard translates strategy into strategic objectives, KPIs, and actions/initiatives.

In one way, Kaplan and Norton have been almost too successful with the KPI part of the balanced scorecard. Although their first book was rather KPI focused, later books have repositioned the scorecard more as a *strategy execution* process, with KPIs as just one part of the model. But the initial KPI success seems to stick too well in many companies. KPIs are now all over the place—not just in business, but increasingly also in public organizations. Any reputable hospital now has a KPI scorecard in place, often with questionable results.

There is nothing wrong with KPIs. They can do great things for us. The problem is that we need *more* than KPIs. They cannot do the job alone. We seem to have forgotten that the "I" in KPI stands for *indicator*. Indicators are meant to measure and give us an *indication* of whether we are moving toward our strategic objectives and delivering on our strategies. This works quite well within the finance perspective of the scorecard. Here the link between strategic objectives and KPIs is normally strong and obvious. If a strategic objective is to increase shareholder value, and the KPI is share price development, the KPI is providing much more than an indication of delivery against the strategic objective.

When we move from the financial perspective to the other ones, the more indicative this relation becomes. Take the example of safety, a very important area for both Borealis and Statoil. A strategic objective might be to achieve a step change in safety performance. Is it a given that this really is taking place, even if a safety KPI such as number of safety meetings held is moving in the right direction? It might be the case, but we cannot determine whether it is based on the KPI alone. We cannot expect these KPIs to tell us the full truth and the whole story. A high fever is a strong indication that something is wrong, but it seldom gives us the full diagnosis.

I have been working with scorecards and KPIs since 1995. For far too long I searched for the perfect KPI. I gave up many years ago. It does not exist. There are many good KPIs, and combinations of KPIs can make them even better. But the perfect one? Forget it.

We need something else in addition to the indications we get from the KPIs. We have to take off our KPI glasses and look at what the KPIs do not pick up. We need to make other observations and use them in a more holistic assessment.

Just Another Command-and-Control Tool

Detailed budgets, supported by consequences people fear if the numbers are not met, are a proven and effective way of tying an organization's hands and feet.

Implementing a scorecard does not necessarily solve this problem. It actually can make things worse. If such a control mind-set remains unchallenged and unchanged, scorecards often are used to tighten the control screw even harder. The budget enables managers to execute *financial* microcontrol only. A scorecard broadens the control menu significantly, into all the other nonfinancial perspectives. It can be used for a detailed and mechanical top-down cascading of strategic objectives, KPI targets, and actions across all perspectives. It is the trust issue again. In addition to sharing and aligning direction through strategy and strategic objectives, the belief is that people must also be instructed in detail about how to get there. Corporate functions such as finance, HR, and HSE often join in, demanding that "their" KPIs and actions on the corporate scorecard be found all the way down to secure "corporate delivery" within their own area. An HR KPI on group level does not necessarily address the broad variation in HR challenges across all front-line units.

A top-down approach does not cause serious damage only to motivation. Wrong decisions might also be made, and good ideas lost, especially when the distance to the front line is long, maps are outdated, and there are surprises hiding around every corner.

As the name states, *balance* is key in a scorecard. I believe there is one balancing act that has not gotten enough attention in the scorecard theory. As we have discussed earlier, we need to find the right balance between:

- Alignment, from strategy to people, from center to front line
- Freedom and flexibility for local teams to sense and respond in their own dynamic environment

The balance is about scorecards used for top-down strategy alignment versus scorecards used as front-line tools for local teams to perform and deliver in their own business reality, including picking up on and responding to issues that not yet may be visible on the corporate radar screen. These two purposes often pull in opposite directions. If the alignment purpose always wins, if a scorecard is perceived as nothing but a landing ground for stuff from above, with no room to move and with no place for local focus and initiatives, then the scorecard risks losing its standing and relevance. If a scorecard gets a feed-the-machine image—something you do for the layers above only—then it is reduced to nothing but an imposed and unpopular reporting exercise. The classic symptom is again when scorecard updating takes place only when it is time for the next business review with the level above.

Of course a scorecard cannot be local only and disconnected from the rest of the company. It has to be a combination of the two, but the *perception* should still tip in favor of local ownership. One way of achieving this is a broad and involving scorecard design process that reflects both purposes. It feels local but has a central origin.

Securing alignment must not be a mechanical exercise. It should take place mainly through a *translation* of strategic

Alignment through strategic objectives

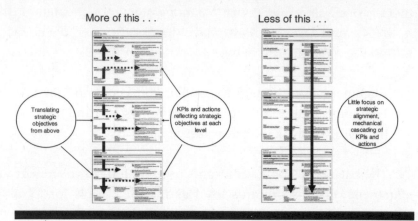

StatoilHydro

EXHIBIT 4.21 Translation vs. Cascading

objectives. KPIs and actions should then be defined based on these translated strategic objectives. Therefore, a mechanical cascading of KPIs and actions should be avoided. Sometimes it might be required, but this should rather be the exception than the rule, as illustrated in Exhibit 4.21.

Only One Scorecard at the Top

Some companies have only one or just a few scorecards. In a small company, this might be fine. In larger organizations, this is seldom enough. It might seem sufficient for top management, giving guidance on overall direction and spelling out targets and high-level initiatives on the company level. But beyond that, what does the scorecard really mean for each of the business areas and for units and people in the front line? All of these areas and units probably have their own budgets. With budgets but no scorecard at these levels, the result is a simple walk-over for the budget mind-set.

I am not saying that all front-line units and cost centers necessarily should have their own scorecard, although that can be a good option here also. The nearest scorecard must be close enough to provide clear guidance and inspiration. It must be perceived as relevant and meaningful at the level at which it is used. That will seldom be the case if people need binoculars to see it.

The analogy of an airplane cockpit sometimes is used to describe the balanced scorecard. I am not sure if I like this way of illustrating the concept. It triggers a number of traditional management associations in me. The captain and the copilot—the CEO and the CFO—are both in the cockpit, surrounded by measurements. They are constantly fed updated information. They watch, analyze, and take decisive actions when lights flash and bells ring. Back in the cabin, the passengers eat, sleep, and kill time waiting for the pilots to bring them safely to the targeted destination. They have limited information, beyond what they can see through small windows and hear in a noisy cabin. Business-class passengers are a bit better informed, as they sit closer to the cockpit door, which from time to time is open. They also find the trip more comfortable than those back in economy class.

Some passengers react on all the instructions from the cabin crew, from those with less impressive uniforms than the guys up front in the cockpit. There seems to be a sharper edge in their voices the farther back in the cabin they move, passing on messages from the cockpit and issuing instructions about seat belts and luggage.

In today's organizations, people no longer accept being passive passengers, leaving their destiny completely in the hands of a few guys on the top. People want to be informed and involved. They do not accept being intimidated by middle managers who believe authority comes from stars and stripes. And people also question too large differences between business and economy class.

A Paralyzing Balance

A scorecard is a much bigger and better radar screen than the financially oriented budget and business plan. The broader focus includes other stakeholders, such as employees, customers, shareholders, and society at large. Through a scorecard, we aim to formulate a cause-and-effect relationship between the different perspectives and stakeholders. How does the organization's learning and development impact our operating processes, which are necessary for the satisfied customers we need in order to produce income and a financial result? Although we are able to define plausible cause-and-effect relations that illustrate how the different perspectives link and support each other, there might still be conflicts between different stakeholder interests. Employees might want higher salary levels, customers might want lower prices, and taxes or restrictions imposed by society might conflict with shareholder interests.

If we want to create sustainable value, we cannot ignore any of the company's stakeholders. At the same time, we cannot aim for simultaneous short-term maximization of all stakeholder interests, which might cause a paralyzing balance. When a scorecard does not sufficiently address choices and priorities, and does not distinguish between today and tomorrow, we risk sending the message that everything is equally important. This might leave the organization in limbo, trying to run after everything at the same time. Again, strategy is about making choices. If you never say no, you do not have a strategy. Choices must be made and also must be clearly reflected in the scorecard.

A final reflection on balance. Sometimes it is actually unbalance that brings movement and progress, like the human body walking. Each step leaves us out of balance, which we handle by taking another step, and another one, and the result is that we keep moving forward.

It Is a Finance Thing

The majority of scorecard projects and operating responsibilities sit firmly in the finance function. One reason is probably that finance is the main number collector in companies and the reporting and control function. In many companies the scorecard process is about just that, so finance is the obvious candidate for the job. Could another function take this job? What about the strategy function, or human resources?

This is the wrong discussion. The main issue is not where to place the responsibility but how the responsible function works together with other functions. Whoever the owner is, a close coordination across traditional functional borders is required. The scorecard process must involve strategy, finance, and HR. It is about *integrated* performance management, from overall strategies and strategic objectives, to KPIs, actions and forecasts; and further into team and personal goals, evaluation, and reward. Close cooperation with IT is also needed, to ensure a continuous and effective development of the scorecard system. IT needs to be on the inside and understand the process, not on the outside delivering on detailed system specifications they do not understand the background for. IT is, however, not a scorecard process owner candidate.

There is, in fact, no perfect candidate for the scorecard job within the traditional functional structure in companies. Obviously, it is a line responsibility, but so is everything. You need a clear owner who drives, coaches, and ensures a continuous development of both process and system. The finance function is probably best positioned for the job, simply because it sits in the middle between strategy and people. But this responsibility takes quite a different mind-set and competence from what we typically find in finance. It requires a holistic perspective, a broad understanding of strategy and organizational behavior, on top of the necessary business and financial competence. Add on communication skills beyond the ability merely to read out the numbers.

Some companies have decided to set up a dedicated unit, as suggested by Kaplan and Norton. The Office of Strategy Management, introduced in their new book, *The Execution Premium*, holds an overall responsibility for the strategy execution process. It is an interesting idea, but it also introduces an additional interface to manage. On balance, I believe a more sustainable solution is to take the longer and more demanding route of growing the finance function into this role. Or maybe a finance/HR alliance could be a solution, as will be discussed later in the chapter.

Sometimes the context in which a scorecard is introduced can do something with the perception of ownership. When PC producer Compaq introduced scorecards several years ago, it also made changes to its bonus system, including a tight link to scorecards. For several years, people talked about scorecards only as "the bonus system."

It Is a Manual Thing

An active and pulsating scorecard process, living from the boardroom to the control room, cannot be based on a manual collection and publication of data. Some kind of system is needed.

Whatever your system choice, it is important not to let the system become a straitjacket for your process design. It might be wise to start out manually on a small scale, maybe with a few pilot tests to learn and improve before a more permanent model is automated. The manual period should not be too long, though, as manual scorecards are demanding to operate and often do not provide the best data quality.

A number of scorecard packages are on the market, ranging from stand-alone systems with varying integration possibilities to scorecard modules in larger enterprise resource planning (ERP) applications. Beyond all the IT-technical issues that someone else must help you with, my advice is to pressure test the system candidates on these points:

- Does the package focus on KPIs only, or does it also have good functionality for handling strategic objectives and actions and other interactive free-text information?
- Is the user interface simple and intuitive, a no-brainer for managers who still have their secretaries print all their e-mails?
- Can you easily add on other information that teams need in their daily jobs, so that the application becomes more of a management information portal?
- Can the system follow you on your scorecard journey? Can you adjust and improve without mobilizing armies of IT people?
- Does the system vendor understand performance management from an organizational point of view or only see it as a mechanical data-collecting and reporting exercise?

It goes without saying that the final decision must lay with the scorecard responsible function and not with IT.

If your system meets all these requirements on top of all the demands coming from your IT colleagues, working with it probably will not be your main challenge. But believe me, there will be enough other challenges!

Joint Venture Budgets

Now we turn to something quite different. This short section is probably of interest only for those working in the oil business. I hope there are at least some of you reading this book! I need to address joint venture budgets because they represent a major Beyond Budgeting barrier for an oil company. For some people, they also represent an excuse for not getting onboard. You might want to skip this section if the oil business is very remote from your line of work.

The exploration and production part of the oil business typically is organized in joint ventures in order to share risk. A joint venture has an operator responsible for daily operations. The operator normally has the highest ownership share. Other partners hold the remaining ownership shares, and together, the owners decide on strategies and other major issues through a joint management committee.

Joint venture agreements typically require the operator to present a work program and a corresponding cost budget for partner approval. Both Statoil and Hydro were major operators on the Norwegian continental shelf, together operating around 80% of Norwegian production. The new company is therefore exposed to such budget requirements in a large number of joint ventures. Many people ask why we bother with abolishing budgets internally when we still are obliged to provide them for these joint ventures.

We believe it still makes sense, for these reasons:

- A significant part of the company is not working toward these joint ventures; this includes, for instance, almost the entire downstream area. In fact, the majority of StatoilHydro employees are not directly affected by joint venture budgets.

- It is worthwhile to make the internal room to move bigger even if we have to act in smaller rooms in the joint ventures. One big room and one small one are better than two small ones.

- A new standard agreement valid for all joint ventures on the Norwegian continental shelf has just been put in place. The budget chapter is still there, but a new and promising chapter requires the operator to establish something that is, for all practical purposes, an Ambition to action. When this agreement begins to work as intended, we hope this will be where the partners have their main focus, simply because it is a more meaningful way to have a dialog and follow-up of the operator than the traditional budget. This might also enable us to harmonize internal and joint venture processes much better than today, which will be good news for everybody, particularly for the partners paying for the operator's work.

- Important parts of the Ambition to action process are also outside the scope of the joint ventures, such as how we internally define and evaluate performance.

Introducing the Ambition to action concept into the joint ventures we operate is on our to-do list, but it is on the back burner; merger integration is job number one.

What Is Next?

We are on a long journey, where the direction is clearer than the destination. The process changes we have been through are summarized in Exhibit 4.22.

You will recognize many of the Beyond Budgeting principles here. As with those 12, the list in the exhibit is not a buffet

A systematic change through the whole process

	From "Annual command and control"	To • **Continuous and dynamic** • **More freedom and responsibility** • **New performance language**
Targets	• Equal to plan "What we can deliver" • KPI targets • Absolute targets	• Aspiration driven: "What we must deliver." Targets before plan. • "Ambition to action" • Relative targets
Plans	• Plan = target, forecast, and resource allocation • Gaps *versus* targets hidden • One outcome only • Very detailed	• Plan = forecast only (actions and *expected* performance) • Gaps *versus* targets visible • Main uncertainty spans • Less detailed
Resource allocation	• Annual preallocation through budgets • Budgets "an entitlement —my money"	• Resources available when needed, but within KPI targets + mandates + decision criteria. Monitoring of development
Business reporting	• Backward looking • Variance *versus* year-to-date budget	• Forward looking • Forecast *versus* targets, and actions to close gaps
Evaluation/ rewards	• Based only on budget figures and KPI targets	• Broader evaluation: "Ambition to action"+ Behavior

StatoilHydro

EXHIBIT 4.22 The Process Changes

menu. It represents a systematic change where all elements hang together and support each other. Take the link between forecasting and resource allocation. What is the point of having the world's largest radar screen and the ability to sense and (try to) respond instantly, if there is no dynamic resource allocation ensuring that the necessary resources also can be instantly accessed or reallocated, instead of being locked up in a detailed annual budget?

Implementing the changes described and realizing the required changes in leadership behavior is difficult for any company. We are still in process and far from declaring any mission complete. But even if our main focus is on implementing what is already decided, we have new thoughts and ideas on the table. These all aim to take Ambition to action to "the next" level. This objective is even found in CFO Eldar Sætre's own Ambition to action. The ideas I present next are not yet ready for approval and launch, but they are gradually moving toward concrete proposals. We have tested some of them in the organization. People are curious, and the response is generally positive. Nevertheless, from some quarters, we are faced with some of the same skepticism we met when we started challenging the budget several years ago.

Dynamic and Event-Based Forecasting?

Rolling forecasts have been implemented in many companies, sometimes as a first cautious step toward a broader Beyond Budgeting model. Some people even believe that Beyond Budgeting *is* about rolling forecasts, which by now you understand is a major misunderstanding. As in most companies, our long-term forecasts have always been rolling, adding on one more year every year. It is the short-term forecasting that still stops at year-end ("forecasting against the wall" as some call it), because we have not yet implemented short-term rolling forecasts. We were just waiting for the moment to take this step also. But something happened along the way. It became more and more apparent that a traditional rolling forecast might not be the right solution for us. We question whether it is possible to force the turbulent reality around us into anything fixed. A five-quarter rolling horizon is of course better than stopping at year-end. But it is still a fixed period, five quarters instead of four. Why is a *five*-quarter horizon the right answer? And why should there be *one* fixed forecasting frequency and horizon for all the different businesses in the company? Our crude oil traders and geologists have very different time perspectives. Why should they all be forced into the same rhythm? The calendar also dictates *when* forecast updates should take place. In Statoil this has typically been every quarter, although production, for instance, is forecasted more frequently. The long-term forecast is an annual autumn exercise. Does it have to be this way?

What if we turn it all around and build our processes around business rhythms and the real world instead? Remember, one of the main purposes of forecasting is to get issues on the radar screen early enough to be able to act. When is the right time to look at your radar screen? Is it at fixed and regular intervals or more continuously? Does sailing in narrow and busy waters and not at open sea make a difference? What is the right size of your radar screen? A supertanker needs a larger one than a speedboat, right?

We have therefore started designing a more dynamic forecasting process, which we want to be more *event* than calendar driven, with no fixed update frequency and no fixed time horizons. We have by no means at all sorted it out yet, but intuitively it feels right.

An event is something that happens around us, which has an effect that we need to reflect in our forecasts. It could also be an action we take ourselves, which we believe will have a forecast impact. We do not think there can be any detailed instructions defining how big an event must be to trigger a forecast update. The main principle might be to include what is relevant for the unit in question. What is a big dot on a local radar screen would often be an ignorable event for the company, but seldom the other way around. The company should therefore always have more than sufficiently updated forecasts.

Another benefit of dynamic forecasting is that studies and analysis triggered by new information would not be piled on top of each other in a busy autumn planning period. By catching these issues when they occur during the year instead, there will be more quality time available for doing the necessary analysis.

Let me make a comparison with accounting or related processes such as order handling or payments. We do not stockpile orders, invoices, and payments and register all of them at month-end, even if the month is the main reporting interval we have chosen. We register continuously, and anyone with a need for more frequently updated information can get it. Even if we have not closed the books, there is a wealth of continuously updated information also available for us in the system during the month, from order status to cash positions and cost development.

There will still be regular milestones when we will tap into the latest forecast to provide data to internal or external stakeholders, such as the board, authorities, partners, and others, in addition to more unscheduled milestones when important events trigger a need for seeing the bigger picture. These milestones should not lead to frenetic activity to update the numbers, because much of the job had been done already. The job should be more about doing some final checks and quality controls. The intention is to move away from the annual planning stint in the autumn, into something more continuous and business driven. The new approach might actually be closer to how the organization already works. Today we analyze the potential from exploration discoveries when the discovery is made. Nobody waits till the autumn. Cost and production forecasts on new field development projects are updated as the project passes decision gates, again a continuous process.

We know, however, that there are several issues we need to address and sort out—such as updating discipline and coordination—but we are pretty sure it must be possible to find ways of handling these issues.

Leaving the Calendar Prison for Good?

The calendar year is an artificial and restricting concept not just for forecasting but for the entire performance management process. In the oil business, hydrocarbons have neither knowledge of nor loyalty to the idea of something called January to December. Although some businesses might have cycles that revolve around summer and winter seasons, we mess it up even here. That winter season is cut in two by December–January. HR is experiencing the same problem. It would be much easier if people changed jobs only at year-end. Anything else complicates the process: personal goals might be messed up, performance dialogs must be taken out of sync, and so forth.

What if we organized ourselves around business cycles instead of calendar cycles in the rest of the Ambition to action process as well, not only in forecasting? What if we left the calendar year behind at every chance possible? What could our processes then look like? It is a simple question but with some mind-blowing consequences once we start exploring what this could mean in practice. But really, how radical of a change would it be? Is it not only common sense, what we would have done if we were not tied down by legacy and tradition?

Let us accept that the statutory and tax accounting will remain calendar based. That is not a show-stopper. Beyond this not too problematic constraint, there is a great potential for major improvements. Let us take a look at what an Ambition to action process could look like if we released it from the calendar prison:

- Our *strategy* process is already continuous and issue driven. *Strategic objectives*, however, could be updated as required, when strategy changes so much that new or revised objectives are needed. This could take place at any time during a year.
- We could select *KPIs* and set *KPI targets* as needed. New KPIs could be triggered by new strategic objectives or simply when we find better ones. KPI targets could be adjusted at any time when there is a need for adjusting the course or the ambition level. The MIS system would keep a log of all changes as needed.
- The *target horizon* and the milestones under way could vary, depending on the type of business and the urgency of what we aim to achieve. The more relative league standings

targets we set, the less need there will be for setting annual targets. "Advancing on the table," "above average," and similar relative targets do not need to be reset every year. External targets toward the market would, however, need to be more stable. The more relative targets we use here, the less of an issue this becomes (e.g., relative ROCE).

- *Actions* are already meant to be continuously updated, but more dynamic strategic objectives and KPIs would make this even more obvious and natural.
- *Forecasting* would be continuous and event driven, as described.
- Based on the new forecasting process, *business reviews* could address shorter- and longer-term issues in a more fluid way than today, driven by the lead time of corrective actions more than calendar periods. This would not necessarily mean mixing strategy with operations, but many operational issues in our business have long lead times. Nor is the distinction between operations and strategy always razor sharp.
- *Performance evaluation* could be more closely linked to completion of projects and activities, catching fresh learning much more effectively. There might be a need for a default regular evaluation because of the annual rewards cycle (or *must* pay reviews always be done once a year for everyone?) Whenever the performance evaluation takes place, it would be against an Ambition to action, which in some cases had changed radically during the year, in other cases very little. It would also become even more obvious that Ambition to action is no fixed performance contract.

Many of you probably came far in making a "But what about...?" list while reading the points above. Our list is also long. We have not got it all sorted out yet, but we believe we can. One of my implementation rules is to "Design to 80%

and jump," sorting out the rest afterward. That advice is highly relevant here as well.

Some people will argue that the organization needs the imposed discipline of a fixed and regular cycle: "If not, things simply will not happen." I can accept that small children and some adults need the predictability of a fixed and regular schedule. But if this is a major problem in an organization, I see it more as a symptom of something else, as a lack of mature and independent leaders and employees who take the initiative as needed. Is the situation really that bad, or could the trust issue be at play here?

Lack of updating discipline might also be a symptom of lack of ownership to the performance management process, which we try to compensate for through discipline enforcement instead of addressing the underlying causes. If people operate their Ambition to action more for themselves than for others, then updating discipline becomes less of an issue because the root cause problem is removed.

We might also see an important development in how we use KPIs, moving from *control* to *learning*. Today we implicitly assume that a KPI on Ambition to action must have a target, although an increasing number of KPI targets are being set by the units themselves and are not imposed from above. Follow-up against targets is a key control mechanism to secure desired performance. In the future, the main purpose of a KPI might be to learn, to help us become better. Targets might become more implicit, with "positive trend," "above average," and similar ambitions as evergreen performance expectations. The purpose is still the same, to achieve the best possible performance, but it would be a process more owned by the teams than imposed from above. By giving priority to learning rather than control, the result might very well be even better performance.

With so many new people onboard after the StatoilHydro merger, it has been necessary to refocus our efforts on communication and explanation of the model. However, I believe that taking the steps described actually would help us in implementing Phase 1 by reinforcing some of the principles in the existing model. One example is planning. Although planning now has a new content and is about actions and their expected consequences, it is still called a plan (a possible mistake). As long as the timing also is autumn (budget time), we experience that the old name and timing reinforces the old mind-set and makes it difficult for some people to understand what is new. By moving to a more event-driven and continuous process, it might become easier to see that the new process is about more than rearranging deck chairs.

Finance and HR: Time for a New Partnership?

Finance and HR are traditionally not the best of friends in companies. Having worked in both functions, I know too well how they talk about each other. It is not very nice either way. They talk a lot *about* each other but not much *with* each other; they hardly communicate, and when they do, they hardly understand each other. Some might see this somewhat hostile relationship as nothing but an innocent and given reality in company life. The consequences can, however, be serious. When HR preaches leadership while finance pushes management, and the two point in completely different directions, the contradicting messages undermine each other and confuse the organization. Most HR people both appreciate and preach the importance of freedom, trust, and transparency. The problem is that they seldom seem to make a reality check against the actual management processes in the company. The budgeting mind-set is a prime example. Their messages become hollow and theoretical. Everybody knows the rules of the game and what really counts. The "hard" finance processes almost always win over the more fragile but well-intended HR messages when the two collide. The terms "hard" and "soft" should, by the way, perhaps be used the other way around. I actually believe being good on HR is much "harder" than a lot of the finance and business issues we like to boast about.

Historically, the two functions have had very separate responsibilities. Finance is coming from a money-dominated history of statutory accounting, taxes, cash management, and so on. HR's legacy is recruitment, employment contracts, welfare, pensions, and the like. Salary administration and travel expenses were for many years the only common ground between the two.

This is, however, changing. In both functions, transactional tasks are being moved over to shared service centers, which enables more focus on a process that has been growing into perhaps the most important one in both functions: *performance management*. The problem is the Berlin Wall right across a process that must run seamlessly all the way into HR territory. I believe we now are reaching a point where finance and HR must join forces around a common performance management process in a much stronger and more formal way. There are three reasons for this.

1. The company and the performance management process need it.
2. Finance needs it.
3. HR needs it.

I will elaborate on these reasons when discussing implementation advice later on, because involving HR has been one of my very positive implementation experiences.

In Statoil, finance and HR have worked closely together on the Ambition to action process. It has not always been like this. Although the two functions are located close to each other at the headquarters, the level of cooperation and mutual respect between the two used to be similar to that found in most companies: not much to write home about.

Direction and business targets were formulated in a strategy-and finance-driven process. When it was time for individual goals, HR took over, sometimes starting almost over again instead of building on what already had been done. The HR chapter in the annual business plan was often a last-minute effort, with great words but varying substance and few implementation thoughts behind it all. I hope my good friends in HR do not feel I am being too hard on them, but it was very much like this. Finance and top management were, however, as much to blame as HR.

Over the last years, the situation has changed a lot. The reason is twofold. First, CEO Helge Lund has been crystal clear since day one on his intentions of lifting HR and people and organization issues high up on the business agenda. Second, the finance–HR channel has been opened. I dare to take at least some credit for this. Heading up HR in Borealis radically changed my view on this function and on the formidable potential available for both functions in a stronger cooperation. I spent many hours in the HR corridors in Statoil when returning from Borealis. Perhaps some were a bit skeptical, but many were curious about this finance guy using their own language and being so interested in their own issues. Whatever the reason, today there is a much better climate and a clear recognition in both functions that stronger cooperation is the only way forward.

The results are visible in several areas. The people process is now much better integrated into the rest of Ambition to action, through an almost seamless transition between business and individual goals. Also, the people and organization perspective in Ambition to action has been completely revitalized, with HR strongly embracing the concept.

The response from the organization is very positive. People understand and appreciate how Ambition to action finds its way into team or individual goals and also how we have broken the mechanical link between targets, evaluation, and bonus.

I believe this cooperation will grow even stronger in the years to come. Personally, I have a dream about this common ground one day developing into something even firmer. Could we even foresee a new organizational function with people from both camps, responsible for the entire performance management process? I would not be surprised to see a number of strategy people also knocking on that door—perhaps even a few communication guys.

And Beyond This?

The Statoil case was the story up until the merger in 2007. The journey continues, but in many ways StatoilHydro is now at the crossroads. I believe the next couple of years will be critical and will determine whether what you have heard about in this chapter was just another management box after all or actually something much bigger.

When we started out in 2005, we did not position the case for change and our proposals as a radical organizational turnaround like Handelsbanken undertook in 1970. Our problem description and proposed solutions mainly addressed quality and efficiency problems and the obvious consequences: replacing traditional budgeting with better processes. For most people in the company, this was, and still is, seen as a radical step. Since then, our focus and agenda have gradually broadened. The budget discussion is still there, but it is much less heated than in the early days and now much more about understanding than about protesting and rejecting. Today our discussions have moved toward issues that would have been no-go zones back then, such as questioning calendar years or individual bonuses. The leadership implications are emerging as a much more natural part of the model. When today we are invited into management teams, leadership training, network meetings, or other communication opportunities, we always position Ambition to action as a leadership philosophy as much as a management process.

The leadership messages resonate well in the organization. Many of the Beyond Budgeting leadership principles are actually quite obvious for us, a young company born and raised in a Scandinavian culture, and well in line with how the company has operated since its birth in 1972, two years after Handelsbanken's rebirth. Although the English language talks about leaders and managers, the Scandinavian languages have just one word: *leder*, as the Norwegian version would read. We actually do not have a word for manager. That might not be a coincidence.

The power distance in the company is short. The actual distance has always been shorter than what it might look like on the organization chart. Hearing the CEO addressed by his first name is as natural as seeing him without a tie. The value orientation has always been strong, which is seen in the intensity of discussions when value statements have been updated. The score on the annual climate survey question asking if people are "proud of the company and would recommend Statoil as an employer to friends and family" has consistently been high. The same goes for whether you "have the necessary influence over your own job." Our local autonomy has always been higher than that of our competitors. At least, that is what people tell us when they join Statoil from these companies. Some might say it has been too high, during heated discussions about harmonization of local back-office processes, which has little to do with the local freedom Beyond Budgeting advocates. Innovation and challenge has been the bread and butter of the company. The transparency mind-set has been there all along, and it is now supported by new and better information systems such as MIS, intranets, and team sites. The company has a long tradition of working through processes and networks that runs across the formal organization chart.

Some people will, however, claim that the characteristics I have just mentioned were even stronger in earlier days. This is probably true and not any nostalgia trip. Something did happen along the way. Some of it has of course to do with size. The company is much larger and more complex today than it was in the 1970s and 1980s. But much also has to do with influences. Western (read U.S./U.K.) influences on management and leadership have been strong in Scandinavia. These have come dressed as both leadership philosophies and as tools and processes. There has been great stuff in both categories, but also the opposite. The Scandinavian culture has been strong enough to resist many of the more questionable leadership influences, but the armor has been thinner on the tools and process side. Maybe the reasoning has been that even though we could see potential negative side effects, our strong culture could handle it. Sometimes we were right, and sometimes not. Process change *influences and drives* culture and behavior more than we think.

Addressing the leadership side of Beyond Budgeting just as vigorously as the process side is critical for achieving real change. Yet our initial *process* focus actually may have been the right place to start. Our cultural background provides us with a better starting point on the leadership side than many other companies born and raised in different cultures. Maybe job number one is to ensure that our processes are organized *on* and not *against* the culture we are coming from and the leadership style we naturally lean toward.

The merger represents a challenge in itself. Five thousand new colleagues coming from Hydro have not been part of the journey so far. Although we share the same national culture, there are some company-culture differences, perhaps related to age and tradition. Hydro has a more than 100-year history. I am, however, optimistic. I have met many new colleagues when presenting Ambition to action in new management teams, at leadership training sessions, and in network meetings. The large majority are positive when they hear the full story, not just the headlines. We must be patient and give everyone a chance to catch up. Just pointing to what the merger agreement says provides little or no motivation for that journey.

Taking the possible next steps into a more continuous and event-driven process will be another important test and milestone. Although many of these steps lie on the process side, these changes probably will also give a strong pull for leadership changes. At a minimum, the deep and radical change we aim for should become even more visible to the organization.

Another challenge already with us is the extreme cost pressure in the industry. The dramatic cost increases on almost everything we purchase has already been used by some as evidence that we lose cost control without budgets. As if steel and drilling rigs would become cheaper if we reintroduced budgets! I believe, however, that there is room for improvement in our activity accounting and also in our cost monitoring.

As Scandinavia's largest company, StatoilHydro has become an even bigger player in Norwegian society after the merger. Even more eyes are closely watching every move we make. Even though we have been presenting our new model at a number of national conferences, the tabloids have not yet had any ignorant headlines: "Stinking Rich Company Now Even Throws Budgets Overboard." Actually, the first front page we got was in a well-respected Norwegian management weekly, which ran a factual and positive five-page story with CEO Helge Lund on the front page. But that other ignorant front page will most likely come one day, and more people read tabloids than management weeklies.

We also seem to get help from unexpected places. I recently became aware of major new movements in product development and project management based on "agile" and "lean" principles; the leading method in this trend is called Scrum. The name comes from rugby—the circle the players form shoulder to shoulder when starting to play.

Scrum is a response to many of the same myths and problems that triggered Beyond Budgeting and that traditional system development has been struggling with for decades. The concept draws on the lean principles pioneered by Toyota, with agility as a key mind-set. Scrum describes the illusion of control in traditional project management by recognizing that system projects also involve high variability or uncertainty with regard to what the users really want, how long it will take, and what it will cost. It recognizes that adaptive processes are needed and challenges the standard assumption that a system project, or any other project requiring innovation and creativity, can be planned like a traditional construction project or run with a predictable-system, manufacturing mind-set. It undresses the traditional "waterfall" (sequential) life cycle, which slices projects in isolated design, build, and test phases with no meaningful iteration, feedback, or learning cycles. Modern research shows that waterfall life cycle projects are correlated with worse failure, productivity, cost, and schedule performance than agile methods such as Scrum.

Scrum is an adaptive process with short time-boxed development iterations (called "Sprints" that typically last two weeks). In each Sprint, the highest-priority (small-size) goals are pulled from a product backlog and developed. At the end of each short iteration, there is a formal inspect-and-adapt step: Business sees the running, tested product increment in a public demonstration; talks with the team; reprioritizes the product backlog based on the latest information; and repeats the cycle. Transparency; early delivery of tangible, high-value goals; time-boxing; and inspect-and-adapt are key themes. In addition, Scrum is based on cross-functional and self-managed teams with no traditional project manager; the team decides how to best meet the Sprint goals and time-box deadline. The team may also "descope" a goal if it is discovered to be more work than estimated, but the time box is never extended; the process consists of fixed time periods of variable scope in short cycles. Scrum embraces flexibility and responding to change rather than following a plan; businesses can change priorities at any two-week Sprint boundary as they learn new insights, though never within a sprint. Another theme is to favor close collaboration over hand-off of voluminous documents; the short cycles, feedback loops, and closer interaction between development teams and business people typically allow for a reduction in detailed written user specifications.

Scrum can demonstrate significant improvements in time, cost, and quality in system development projects. The Statoil-Hydro IT function is fully embracing the concept. Maybe the finance-HR alliance just got a new partner on the Beyond Budgeting journey.

Longer term, we also need to make progress on the joint venture budget issue. This is a barrier, real or not, for a number of people close to that part of the business. It is a tough one, with many rather conservative international oil companies present on the Norwegian continental shelf where we have most of our operator roles. My hope is that even if we still need to operate with joint venture budgets, we will be able to make Ambition to action the relevant focal point for operator-partner discussions and follow-up.

I also believe that we need to think differently about Ambition to action and individual goals. As you will recall, individual *delivery* goals are either sourced directly or translated from Ambition to action. The intention has been to strengthen the performance culture by being more explicit about individual delivery expectations. The purpose is OK, even if I question whether the answer is more individual emphasis. There is, however, another important issue here. When Ambition to action lives and breathes throughout the year (and, it is hoped, even more so in the future), it is almost impossible for the many individual delivery goals in the My Performance Goals to follow. The more concrete and detailed we make the hundreds of thousands individual goals that are translated from Ambition to action, the more difficult it is to keep all the MPGs updated. They might actually become the kind of straitjackets budgets often are: very detailed and specific and difficult to adjust when circumstances change. The more activity-oriented individual goals are, the more relevant the budget comparison is. It is almost as if we on the finance side are meeting HR in the doorway, on their way into a room we are leaving because it is too small. There is also the issue of individual versus team goals. As you will recall from the bonus discussion, there is less and less truly individual performance in today's interlinked organizations and complex environments.

A simple way out of this problem is to consider the closest Ambition to action as *team delivery goals* for everyone in the unit and to drop any further split into individual goals. Concrete actions may still carry individual responsibilities, as they already do on Ambition to action. Such team goals would of course be common and public, while most individual delivery goals today are private, even if they rooted in a public Ambition to action. *Behavior* goals should probably be kept as they are today, individual and private, although behavior also is a team issue, not just a private one. One day I hope we might be ready to let go on secrecy here as well.

This approach will require additional Ambition to actions farther out in the organization. The nearest one must be close enough to provide meaning and direction for individuals. Done for the right reasons and used in the right way, an increased number of Ambition to actions would only be positive. Looking at our own Ambition to action, I do not think anyone on our team would be in doubt about direction, tasks, and responsibilities even if there was no additional breakdown into individual goals.

Bonuses are another area where I hope to see change. We have neutralized many of the negative bonus effects by breaking the mechanical link to targets through the holistic assessment, and the size and reach is also relatively modest. I still dream of the company one day having the guts to say good-bye to individual bonuses altogether, for the reasons discussed earlier. Many of my colleagues tell me we will never see that day. They may be right, but the same was said about budgets five years ago.

Finally, I hope to see a collective executive committee even more visible and passionate about the journey, *all* together in the driver seat. We have strong and invaluable support from both CEO and CFO. This will be even more important as we now move forward on the leadership and process front. The finance and HR community must still play a key role, but we will never fully succeed before every StatoilHydro employee can see that the new thinking is something *everybody* in the executive committee not just approves and supports but also drives with conviction and passion.

How Are We Doing?

Everything described in this chapter, whether implemented or ahead of us, has only one purpose: to improve the performance of the company. That point should be pretty obvious, but it is easy to become blinded by all the bells and whistles in our performance management processes and forget the underlying reason for it all.

Russel L. Ackoff had a wonderful metaphor illustrating this point in an article in Wharton Magazine back in 1977. He compared all the efforts put into planning and budgeting in companies with a ritual rain dance, where finance functions seem more interested in improving the quality of the dance than on any impact on the weather. It is natural that you ask the same question: Does it work, or is it just better singing and dancing? Are we performing better?

The question is just as difficult to answer as it is fair to ask. To be honest, we do not know, at least not yet. We have not been on this journey long enough to draw any meaningful conclusions. Changes in leadership behavior will yield the largest benefits, not the process changes, whose main purpose is to drive these leadership changes. Sustainable change in leadership behavior does not and shall not happen overnight. We know, however, that we have solved much (but not yet all) of the quality and efficiency problems. We set better targets and make better forecasts, and we have a more effective resource allocation. We spend less time on number crunching and historical deviation explanations. All of this indirectly supports better performance, but as you will hear about in the next chapter, the performance problem cluster is the most serious one, with the highest potential for improved company performance. The jury is therefore still out.

If we define performance in relative terms (and we should), then our main challenge is not about major performance improvement but more about holding the fort. We have been performing pretty well against the competition for many years already on growth, profitability and value creation.

We have actually not spent much time trying to prove the business case for our Beyond Budgeting journey. This is in part due to the reasons I have listed, but also because there are some things a company should do because it believes and knows they are the right things to do. I seldom hear the bottom-line effects of improving ethical or safety standards being questioned, simply because we know those effects exist. They come as positive contributions or, more often, through prevention of negative effects. As we say in the oil business, if you think safety is expensive, try an accident. The same is true for ethics.

I am convinced that the future will bring more Beyond Budgeting cases and more research on the positive value creation effects of the concept. In the meantime, we simply need to trust the great Handelsbanken case as well as the strong indications coming from newer cases, such as Southwest Airlines, American Express, Ahlsell, Millipore, Aldi, and the many other early movers who have dared to jump based on strong beliefs without waiting for the detailed and bulletproof business case.

CHAPTER 5

Making the Change: Implementation Advice

This advice on Beyond Budgeting implementation is based on lessons learned in both Borealis and Statoil. It is partly about what we got right in the two projects, but also about the mistakes we made and things we now realize we should have done differently. I do not claim to have all the answers on the right way to go Beyond Budgeting. I doubt if anyone has. Every company is different and has to choose its own way, guided by Beyond Budgeting principles. However, the advice I would like to share will be relevant for many. The seven guidelines are:

1. Creating the case for change
2. Handling resistance
3. Design to 80% and jump
4. Involve human resources (HR)
5. A pull-based and company-owned implementation
6. One war but a thousand battles
7. Do not become a fundamentalist

Creating the Case for Change

Steve Morlidge uses this simple formula to illustrate what it takes to create change:

$$\text{Dissatisfaction} \times \text{Vision} \times \text{Next steps} > \text{Resistance}$$

Any change needs a combination of:

- Dissatisfaction with the current situation
- A compelling vision of an alternative
- The first clear steps toward the vision

The higher the resistance, the higher the product of the three elements on the left side of the equation must be. If any are missing, the case for change is zero. Remember that it is always more fun and more effective to work on the left-hand side. The levers available on the resistance side are fewer. Shooting people is not an option!

The case for change is critical. If an organization or a management team does not understand the fundamental problems with traditional management and the damage they cause, there will be limited appetite for what the alternatives might be and for trying out any. Just because some of the symptoms or smaller parts of the problem are observed and understood does not mean it will lead to a sustainable case for change. Everyone knows that *something* is wrong. But these glimpses of problem understanding alone are not enough to create the dissatisfaction level necessary to go for radical change.

In the beginning of this book, we reviewed a number of problems with traditional management. Many of them are different in nature and therefore require different implementation strategies. We can group some of them in a problem cluster we might call the *performance* problem, because the damage they cause impacts company performance much more severely than, for instance, the efficiency problem (wasting too much time and energy). Within the performance problem, we can include problems about trust, cost management, target setting, evaluations, and bonus. They all have a lot in common. We can also combine the quality problem (conflicting purposes) with the rhythm problem. They both address logic or, rather, lack of logic. We use these problem categories when discussing implementation:

- Performance problem (trust, cost, targets, evaluation, bonus)
- Quality problem (conflicting purposes, rhythm)
- Efficiency problem

The efficiency problem is the easiest to describe and get across. Anyone with a minimum of experience in corporate life knows that the budget process consumes much more time and effort than it deserves. If even this obvious fact should be disputed, it is relatively easy to document by estimating how many hours the process actually consumes. Many external surveys confirm the problem. Several companies are offering benchmarking services on administrative processes such as budgeting and planning. Remember the Hackett Group's finding that the budget process on average consumes 25.000 man-days per billion USD turnover.

The problem with building a case for change just around the efficiency problem is that it is by far the *smallest* problem. If solutions and new processes are designed with this problem as the only basis, there is a risk that the two other and far more important problem areas will be untouched and the enormous potential they represent will remain untapped.

In the ideal world, we would be able to create a full and thorough understanding and acceptance of all three problem areas before moving on to solutions and implementation. Everyone would grasp both the full problem and the full scope of what we are aiming for, even if this end game makes "big hairy goals" look like simple walks in the park.

Unfortunately, very few companies enjoy the luxury of such a starting point. One reason is that Beyond Budgeting still is relatively new. Until the consulting world moves in full scale, making Beyond Budgeting as politically correct as having a balanced scorecard, I am afraid the case for change must be fought one by one. Until then, it will still be an uphill battle, a guerrilla war with a small but committed and hard-fighting group of freedom fighters up against an overwhelming army of tradition, skepticism, and aversion to change.

Should we surrender, if people only are able to get their heads around the efficiency problem? Absolutely not, but I strongly recommend trying to broaden the initial case for change to include at least some of the other problem areas. Try to get the organization to understand and accept parts or the whole of either the performance problem *or* the quality problem, in addition to the efficiency problem. Which one to go for first depends on what kind of organization you are in.

The performance problem is by far the most serious one and *must* be addressed at some point. In an organization dominated by engineers, finance people, and a lot of logical, rational thinking and problem solving, it might be wise to start with the quality problem. The simple fact that an ambitious target cannot be the same number as a 50/50 forecast has a mathematical ring to it. That a cost forecast which doubles as a request for resources seldom will be a good forecast is so obvious that most people get it right away. It is simple to explain and can be illustrated easily with concrete examples from actual budget and planning cases in the company. Add on some calendar examples from the rhythm problem. The light will go on, and people will see something they always have sensed but not fully understood.

The performance problem can be more difficult to get across. When you explain that traditional management and budgets stifle innovation, prevent rapid response, and block good performance, many managers are likely to nod in agreement but think you are wildly exaggerating. And even if they accept that you are right, it is someone else's problem anyway.

There is an interesting pattern in the responses to the performance problem. Leaders and managers respond differently. *Leaders* typically buy into the performance problem, while *managers* more easily embrace the quality problem and also put more emphasis on the efficiency problem compared to their leader colleagues. If you are lucky enough to have many leaders in influential positions, it might be wise to front-load the performance problem. Unfortunately, managers still make up the large majority in most companies, and the performance problem often is the last one to be addressed. But you must not and cannot ignore this problem, even if it is the most difficult one to get across and to do something about. Because it is the most serious problem, it also has the highest payback once addressed and tackled.

You can also structure your implementation more directly around the 12 Beyond Budgeting principles. The recommendations given still will be relevant. Whichever strategy you choose, you will find that the process and leadership principles are closely interlinked and cannot be addressed separately. Process change drives leadership change and vice versa. The effect is even stronger if the process change is introduced and explained not in an isolated and mechanical way, but with equal emphasis on the underlying intentions and leadership implications. What seldom works is communicating leadership changes only, without any supporting process change. Principles like transparency and autonomy cannot just be declared, without immediate, visible, and credible support from corresponding process changes.

Whatever order you go for, in practice the exercise will never be a nicely structured and sequential one. Assume that you start out with the efficiency and quality problems. When a critical mass is onboard and understands these two areas, you move into the design and implementation phase. The fear of the unknown will fade. The comfort level and enthusiasm will increase, because people realize that there actually are ways out of the misery. They discover solutions they believe actually can work. Involvement is critical in this phase. The organization must own the solutions. Blind copying from theory or other companies can easily backfire.

Already at this stage you can start planting the first seeds of the performance problem. Do it gradually and cautiously, using examples from your own company whenever possible. The performance problem is a collection of problems around related principles and processes. Start with the one that is most broken in your company, whether that is the trust problem, the cost management problem, or any of the others.

When moving into solutions, be careful not to oversell. That will only lead people to expect too much too soon. Remember Steve's change formula. Balance your vision and the next steps with the resistance you face.

Former Handelsbanken chief financial officer Lennart Francke has a great metaphor on Beyond Budgeting implementation choices: "Picture a busy London street. Could you imagine the U.K. changing from driving on the left to driving on the right by starting with buses one month, trucks the next, and finally the cars?"

The ideal starting point is of course a full and unanimous support for the entire Beyond Budgeting model. Getting the whole management team onboard is a huge task, though. Even when top management understands it all and wants it all, implementation will still be a long and phased journey. And even if it is possible to synchronize all process changes in a common launch and a big bang, the implementation will not be over before the understanding and acceptance of process changes has been translated into a corresponding change in leadership behaviors. This is a long-haul change, not a quick fix.

So, even if we switched the traffic from left to right overnight, as Sweden did in 1967, we would still see people driving on the wrong side of the road for many years to come. Some would do so because they simply disagree with the change and refuse to switch. Others simply would forget themselves from time to time, without any bad will involved.

As long as they are few, these ghost drivers are not as dangerous as real ones in real traffic. Over time, this kind of driving is of course not acceptable, and such drivers must be brought in line or have their licenses confiscated. But it is unavoidable that there will be a transition period where things will look messy. Many people will be confused because there are old and new behaviors on the street every day. But remember, if there is no mess and no confusion, we are not seeing any real change, just a bit of singing and dancing to the latest music in the charts.

A green light from the board is often seen as absolutely critical for getting started. I do not necessarily see it that way. It depends, of course, on what kind of board you have and on the size of the company. In a large company, with a professional board that understands its governance role (which is not about micromanagement), initial board blessing is not that critical. At some stage, however, board members must be included, but not necessarily from the very beginning.

As you will recall from the Borealis case, we chopped out the calendar year from the rolling financial forecast and shipped it off to the owners, providing them with numbers for their own budget process. Doing this created a bit of extra work in later reporting, but fortunately this was not on a very detailed level. Most of the board members were quite intrigued by what we did, although they all came from budgeting companies.

In Statoil, for several years we provided the board with scorecard-type information in addition to budgets and budget reports. The transition to budgetless reporting was therefore not that big a deal for the board members. I am, however, still impressed with how they welcomed and understood the new process and how disciplined they were in not falling back to budget-type questions. This is especially true since approving budgets and asking difficult questions about budget deviations is what makes many board members feel they are part of the action, with a hand on the steering wheel.

In December 2007, a few months after we went live, the StatoilHydro board approved the new company's first Ambition to action. Even though the board had a number of new members, not a single budget question was asked.

In February 2008 Svein Rennemo was elected new chairman of the board in StatoilHydro.

Handling Resistance

What follows has been learned from years of doing exactly the opposite of what is advised here.

This is about how to tackle all the skeptics you will meet. There will be many of them, and some will offer no support whatsoever for these crazy new ideas. They are convinced that anarchy will follow, costs will explode, and people will misuse their new freedom to run off and do stupid things, like sailors in foreign harbors after months at sea.

As I think back over too many discussions with these guys, a clear pattern emerges. Almost without exception, they all belonged firmly in the *manager* camp. I can hardly remember having these discussions with anyone from the smaller *leader* camp.

In the early days in Borealis, we spent a lot of energy trying to convince these guys that they were wrong. The problem was that we had no evidence, so our discussions were not very constructive. I have now stopped having these discussions, even if I probably forget myself from time to time. I have stopped, simply because it does not work, and it is not worth it. If people are fundamentally skeptical, you cannot talk them into changing their minds, at least not before going live.

Instead, I recommend the opposite. Tell the skeptics that they may be right. It might not work. Costs might increase. We might lose "control." This is a possible scenario. Accept that it might happen. Because they have been listened to and having received that admission from you, the skeptics are now more open for accepting that there might also be a scenario where it actually works, since companies out there have both tried and succeeded.

After agreeing on these two scenarios, move on to the consequences of each one. Start with the failure case. If we fail, totally and miserably, what are really the negative consequences for the company? Remind them that you can go back to budgeting overnight. Nobody will have forgotten how to do it. We do not need to burn or delete old procedures and instructions before we jump. Maybe the next job will not be that interesting for the few who stuck their heads out. Most skeptics will not count that as a negative consequence; rather the opposite. But beyond this, what is really the big risk for the company?

Then ask the skeptics to compare the failure case with the other scenario, the success case. *If* we should succeed, although they will insist the chance is slim, are there any potential benefits? How does it look in companies that have already jumped? How do these benefits compare to the negative consequences of a failure? This line of argument tends to calm the skeptics. You do not convince them, but it all becomes less scary and a bit more acceptable to try out. "But I still don't think it will work!" they will insist. Do not worry. Let them have the last word, and move on.

Sometimes you realize that you have reached skeptics more deeply than you thought. I will never forget a meeting with a new StatoilHydro team shortly after the merger. Naturally, there were a few skeptical comments from some ex-Hydro managers who by then had heard little but the Beyond Budgeting headline. I was explaining dynamic resource allocation when an ex-Statoil manager in the audience suddenly took over, passionately describing and defending the new way of managing costs. I could hardly believe my own ears; this was a guy I had spent hours with trying to convince. Now I could just lean back and leave the floor to him. He was great; I could not have explained things better myself.

Design to 80% and Jump

The only thing you will know for certain about implementation is that there will be challenges and there will be problems. The only thing you do not know is where they will be. Of course you need to plan, design new processes, and try to think through where the risks are and what can happen. But you actually need to apply a Beyond Budgeting principle onto the Beyond Budgeting implementation itself. When entering new and unfamiliar territory, there will be surprises. Not everything can be planned. What is needed is the ability to sense and respond, to act fast and do the right thing when the unexpected hits. This is actually not that difficult as long as the philosophy is understood and the direction is clear.

As you will recall from the Borealis case, we spent a lot of design efforts in the cost control area, because this was where we believed the toughest challenges would be. Instead those challenges popped up in the forecasting quality area.

Another risk of spending too much time on process design up front is that it detracts from the time you could have spent on creating problem understanding, sharing the underlying leadership philosophy, and building the case for change. The more the organization understands the new direction and what we really aim to achieve, the better platform and guidance they have for behaving the right way and making the right decisions in areas where the new process is not perfect from day one.

I would have loved to try out a Beyond Budgeting implementation where almost everything related to traditional management and budgets was removed and nothing else put in place instead, and then just go for it. No targets, no forecasting, no calendars, no micro-instructions, no bonuses. After a year we would take stock and check what we really missed. I would not be surprised if that list turned out to be pretty short.

Involve Human Resources

One of my regrets in Borealis was that HR was involved too little and too late. For many reasons this was not an issue at the time. I had not yet had my debut in HR. Also, my understanding of what kind of journey we had begun was narrower and more financially oriented than it is today. I am convinced that both the model and the implementation would have benefited greatly from having HR onboard earlier.

Many of my finance colleagues cannot understand why I bang on about involving HR. They probably explain it by saying that I am sympathizing with HR because I spent four years in the function. I do sympathize. I learned a lot that you do not learn in finance roles, not even in leadership roles. I got to know a lot of great HR people, and also a few who perhaps should have done something else—just like in the finance function. But that is not the issue. As you will recall, there are three other and more important reasons why HR must be onboard:

1. The company and the process need HR involvement.
2. Finance needs it.
3. HR needs it.

The first point has to do with *integrated* performance management. Ask a finance person for a definition of performance management. I guarantee the answer will include words like "strategies," "budgets," "business plans," "scorecards," "reporting," and the like. An HR person will respond very differently, discussing individual goals, development plans, coaching and feedback, motivation and rewards. They are both right, but they only see their own part of the process. All they list is about performance management, and has to connect, from strategy to people. If you are based outside of finance and HR, as most people in organizations are, you do not care who is responsible for what. You simply want things to hang together, to be consistent and reflect the same management and leadership principles.

So HR must be onboard, to ensure that the new performance management process is integrated and consistent, all the way from strategies and business goals to individual goals and rewards.

The second reason for HR to be involved is that finance needs it. Beyond Budgeting is a massive change project, where we need to go much further than merely changing management processes. We must also find our way into people's hearts and minds. We are seeking deep and radical change in leadership attitudes and behavior. The change is about much more than taking away a budget and implementing a scorecard or a forecasting process, which is where the finance community has its core competencies. When we move outside this comfort zone, we need help from people with skills and knowledge in all those other areas we are trying to reach with Beyond Budgeting. These people are often found in HR. It happens to be their job!

The third reason is important for HR. Today, most HR functions state in their strategies and plans the ambition of becoming a *business partner*. This is a great ambition, but it also is completely unrealistic unless HR becomes more interested in what happens in the performance management process *before* it reaches traditional HR territory. The business partner ambition is also an argument for finance and HR to join forces. How many business partners does the business actually want and need?

Whatever cooperation we talk about, it has so far been more of an exception than a rule. In most companies on a Beyond Budgeting journey, HR has not woken up and finance has not been ready to open the door. We are clearly in the very early phases of something that I strongly believe can grow into a powerful partnership.

A Pull-Based and Company-Owned Implementation

Most large companies suffer from change fatigue. And no wonder. Constant waves of new corporate projects and initiatives roll over organizations. They all have fancy names and well-structured implementation schedules, backed by armies of consultants and a few business hostages as project managers and steering committee members.

You always get a warning. May 12 at 11 o'clock they will knock on your door. The implementation locomotive has reached your unit. They expect you to be motivated and prepared, drop everything else, and make *this* one your number-one priority. Forget the fact that the last team has just left, and you are still digesting the changes those guys rolled in. I am sure you can name a project or two like this that has hit your own unit over the last couple of years.

In Statoil, we chose a different approach for our Beyond Budgeting implementation. We decided on two simple principles:

1. No consultants: We will do it ourselves.
2. No fixed implementation schedule: We will go where the pull is.

The decision to go without consulting support was helped by the fact that I had some previous experience from Borealis. But there we had the same strategy. We did not ask Gemini Consulting to help; it probably could not have done so. We wanted to do it ourselves.

I am not saying that consultants never should be used. A good consultant working behind or alongside you, and not in front of you, can absolutely make a positive difference. As we have discussed, so far consultants have not been very visible in the Beyond Budgeting arena. When they wake up, and if you want help, make sure you choose someone who understands the full picture and is not only in the box-pushing business. Watch out especially for those who wrap it all as nothing but rolling forecasts.

A good alternative is to talk to other companies that are ahead of you. The Beyond Budgeting Round Table is a great place to make such contacts. An increasing amount of literature is available, books and articles. So far most of these have been written with an outside-in perspective and thus they seldom touch the many practical implementation issues. I hope this book will help fill that gap.

Our implementation schedule did include the important milestone of getting the green light to go ahead and when to start out at company and business area levels. But beyond that, in the many business units across the company, we basically followed a strategy of going where the pull was, where there was an appetite for change. This included asking for units that wanted to volunteer as pilots. Three pairs of hands went up fast: our shared services unit, our global exploration unit, and a downstream unit called Nordic Energy.

After these pilots had started, more hands went up. We got invitations from an increasing number of management teams, finance teams, and eventually HR teams. We advanced on the battlefield every day, but more in a guerrilla style than with massive forces. There was no detailed master plan. We went where hands went up and there was an opening. We did not spend much time going for the enemy strongholds. Our strategy was to surround the resistance, not start with it. There was always enough demand to keep us busy. The openings sometimes came as positive surprises, in places we had expected to be closed for quite some time.

I have lost count of all the management teams we have visited over the last three years. We have talked ourselves onto the agendas of leadership development programs, management conferences, and other arenas where leadership and management are discussed. One year I was only a guest at the annual HR conference; the next year I was a speaker.

The process probably looks a bit messy and unstructured from the outside and maybe from the inside as well. The route might seem like a longer one than a more conventional and structured implementation approach. Yet I am convinced that this is a better way of anchoring both the philosophy and the process, making the new model more robust against the unavoidable counterattacks from the "dark forces." Do not be fooled just because they remain still and silent. They will be with us for a long time.

One final piece of advice: Bury the word "roll-out" in a place where it can never be found again. When you say "roll-out," the organization hears "roll over." And guess why? You also may want to bury "cascading" in the same place. Out there it sounds like a bucket of water is about to be thrown at you.

One War but a Thousand Battles

Going Beyond Budgeting sometimes feels like conquering the mountains around my winter cottage in Norway. You aim for a peak in the distance and work hard to get there, only to discover that there is another and higher one behind it. You make it to that one as well, only to see another one and another one. When we got the green light from the executive committee in 2005, I was very much aware that this was only the beginning. It was an important milestone but far from any victorious end.

It was not difficult to climb the immediate next hilltop, to implement the new principles between the executive committee and the business areas right below. They all welcomed the new model with open arms. It gave them more freedom and flexibility, a more meaningful performance language, and less work. But despite the warm welcome, it was hard for some of them to pass on the new-won freedom farther out in the organization: "*We* can of course be trusted. The guys below, though...."

Beyond Budgeting is not something a management team can digest rapidly. You must go through more or less the same phases with each team, at each organizational level. There are, of course, economies of scale, but everyone needs his or her own journey. Each team must be helped through its own case for change: How do the traditional management problems affect our unit? How do we have to change, both on leadership and processes? What does it all mean for us? This must be done level by level. An executive committee decision is necessary but not sufficient. It is a long and hard climb despite the backing of a formal decision, and from time to time it will be tempting to resort to a little dose of command and control. But it works poorly. You can instruct people to make budgets and practice traditional management. You cannot instruct them to stop.

Do Not Become a Fundamentalist

People often ask if the word "budget" now is forbidden. Of course it is not. But we do ask people to try to avoid using it, simply because it can confuse. If we say "budget," what do we actually mean: a target, a forecast, a resource allocation? Nor is keeping a piece of paper in a drawer or a spreadsheet on a PC that looks like a budget forbidden. If people need this safety net in a transition period, then it is not a problem. But we will not consolidate those numbers, and we will not report against them. Over time, we hope and believe that people will find out that perhaps it is not worthwhile spending time on creating these safety nets. But they have to find this out for themselves.

Closing Remarks

There is strong interest for the Statoil and StatoilHydro case in Norway, in Europe, and increasingly outside Europe. We are invited to share our story at numerous conferences and for management teams in other companies. Several case studies have been written about us. In 2007 Statoil was inaugurated into the Balanced Scorecard Hall of Fame, a prize established by Kaplan and Norton. Borealis got the same prize back in 2001.

The ultimate judge is, however, the teams and the people in the company. All the positive feedback we get here is what really counts and is what gives us the energy to climb that next hilltop. At the same time, we are careful with too much victorious celebration. We are still implementing. There are still people in the company who do not believe in the model. We still see managers paying lip service to the new principles. Those are more dangerous than the openly critical ones, with whom you can have a discussion. There are also people working so close to the smaller joint venture room that they feel the new model hardly reaches them. And there are still those who claim that this is all nice theory, because they have not seen much change in their own manager's behavior. So there are still many hilltops to climb.

We all have our bad days. I cannot count many, but there are occasions when the "dark forces" come out of hiding, or you listen to someone you thought was onboard whose words indicate the very opposite. I have a simple and effective remedy for those days: I just think back on where we stood five years ago and compare it to where we are today. If we make equal progress over the next five years, we will have moved mountains. For me, that medicine provides instant and effective relief every time. A comparison with what we aim for on values and ethics might be relevant, because that goal is also very much about change in leadership and behavior. From time to time, and perhaps more often than we like, we all observe colleagues who cross the lines set out in our values and ethical principles. How should we react to this? Should we give up, or should we rather roll up our sleeves and work even harder on what we believe in? For me, there is no question about the right path to take.

As for the model, it is not perfect. We do not have all the answers. We are on a journey where I am certain only about two things: We are heading in the right direction, and what we do tomorrow will be different and better than what we do today. The direction is clearer than the destination, if there is one. Maybe this journey has no end. There is always a better way.

Our energy level is, however, higher than ever. We *know* this is right and good for the company. We *know* other companies will follow. Beyond Budgeting may be the most important new vision out there today, among the myriad of ideas about leadership and management being offered.

My role in StatoilHydro continues my role in Statoil: head of performance management development. I look forward to the journey with my many new colleagues from Hydro. I am convinced they will bring additional experience and perspectives. Together, I hope we will move even closer toward that strategic objective on our own Ambition to action: A leading company on performance management.

In the early pages of this book, I warned you that I would do some shouting and make things as black and white as necessary to get my points across. My apologies if I sometimes seemed too passionate and emotional. It is hard not to, on such big and important issues. If I did, I hope you were able to hear through the noise. I hope you found something to get you started on your own journey or to help you if you already are on the move. Maybe we will bump into each other at one of the many crossroads a Beyond Budgeting journey has to pass. Thank you for listening, and fare well on your own journey, wherever you are coming from and wherever you are heading.

Index